D1488035

EVERYTHING
MATTERS

How a Corporate Over-Achieving Couple
Found Real Truth and How You Can Too

(and it's not what you think)

DENNIS + KATHY LANG

Copyright © 2018 Dennis & Kathy Lang
All Rights Reserved.

CreateSpace Publishing Company
North Charleston, South Carolina

ISBN-13: 978-1719441155

Author Photo by Seth Langner.

Book Design by Matthew Morse.
www.HeyMatthew.com

Praise for *Everything Matters*

"*Everything Matters* recounts a couple's radical transition from a world out of control to a place of physical and mental balance through the practice of yoga. The revelations that occur on the yoga mat permeate their marriage, work life, and relationship with the natural world. Narrated jointly, with a careful attention that is powerfully hypnotic, *Everything Matters* serves as a guidebook for anyone seeking change. Pack your mat. The journey starts here."

Nadine Terk, artist, and Dr. Mitchell Terk, Terk Oncology

"As I try to declutter my life and my mind, I contemplate this notion that everything matters. The Langs have created a powerful expression of understanding how one can let go of things that don't serve you on the journey, yet still appreciate the value they once held. This book will be a companion for years to come, I feel certain."

Kristi Barlow, U.S. Administrative Law Judge

"Within minutes of meeting Dennis and Kathy Lang, most people say 'What do they have / know? I want some!' This amazing book allows the Langs to share their secret. They understand that the truth is not theirs to keep and want to share all they have learned since giving up their fast-paced lifestyle. This book is a game-changer. It will teach you how to live life authentically, to be 'rich' in the fullest meaning of the word. "

Patty Mohler, LMHC

"Dennis and Kathy Lang teach yoga, but in this book—with passion, expertise, and a sense of fun—they take the reader along on their personal journey as they let yoga teach and transform them. How does a corporate, globe-trotting power couple become a lit-from-within teaching team? Here's the story. And you couldn't have better guides to yoga or life."

Judith Leroux, CCht, Clinical and Transpersonal Hypnotherapist, and Denny Leroux, musician and owner of Storm Music Studio

"I feel incredibly honored to know Dennis and Kathy, as their love and gentleness shine forth in their physical practice, their teaching and now this amazing book! To watch their lives unfold paralleling their Yoga is a beautiful sight and I wish everyone inspiration from reading this. And I am so delighted to see they have found their voice!"

Stephanie Keach, Founder and Owner of Asheville Yoga Center

"From its first page, I sensed that *Everything Matters* was written specifically for me—right now. Regardless of how many books you've read on yoga, meditation, or life, this book offers something timely, unique, and important. What lingers is profound gratitude for the realization that every word I speak or think, every thought, feeling and emotion I have, every breath I take, every action, reaction, and inaction, matters greatly. This is not simply a self-help book; it is an authentic invitation and accessible guide to the full cupboard of life—to *be* yoga."

Tarah Trueblood, JD, MA, MDiv.

"Having known Dennis and Kathy for over twenty years, watching their journey from successful and driven leaders in their field to current-day yoga teachers who focus on how we all need to embrace a holistic approach to our lives, is nothing less than transformative and inspiring. They remind us that, while 'we tend to live most of our awakened experiences disconnected from the present,' that's not a permanent state of being if we don't want it to be. Instead, we can embrace their call to 'everything matters' and think of how our actions, the way we ponder our role in society, and even our approach to food can have wider implications 'for the betterment of the world and all beings around us.' Their story is very personal to me, having lived a high-flying corporate lifestyle, focusing only on the material, which spiraled into a world of decadence and had an awful ending, including the loss of liberty. But, as they demonstrate, we don't need an external force to change direction and hit the pause button—to change our trajectories, our health, our lifestyles, and to truly appreciate the gift of each day."

Richard Bistrong, CEO, Front-Line Anti-Bribery LLC

"For those on a journey to spiritualize their lives in a culture focused on materialism, Kathy and Dennis Lang offer guidance based upon their own experience of leaving behind the corporate world to seek deeper fulfillment and a more authentic source of happiness. Their candor about their own experiences makes this book accessible and relatable as they share valuable tools they have gained through the study, practice, and teaching of yoga. It is an excellent bridge for those exploring yoga as a spiritual science and how to integrate it living in the world."

Ruth Hartung (Sraddhasagar), owner and director of *7 Centers Yoga Arts*

"Dennis and Kathy have written a masterpiece from the heart that chronicles their personal transformation using yoga and its teachings as a guide. Their straight-forward explanation of yoga helped me to finally understand it. *Everything Matters* is packed with pearls of wisdom they have learned along the way and contains lots of real world applications and references for people looking for some how-to. I highly recommend it!"

Keith R. Holden, M.D., author of
The Power of the Mind in Health and Healing

"Kathy and Dennis share that they felt a *responsibility* to an inner call to write this book. Anyone who picks it up is, indeed, a very lucky recipient of their unique *ability* to *respond* to that summon. It is to the great benefit of all that this couple applied their years of meditative discipline and yogic skill, as well as their generous hearts, to teach and show that, indeed, everything matters."

Woody Winfree, author of *Lifecycle Celebrant* and
Home Funeral Guide and Sacred Passage End-of-Life Doula

"If you are, like me, on a yoga sojourn, or you know someone who is, get this book! In it, you will discover understanding, context, and guidance. A rich tapestry of yoga fact and background is interspersed in conversation with two wonderful individuals, together an awesome couple, whom I met in their corporate careers and have had the joy of reconnecting with, now, in our mutual yoga years. This book will be a reservoir from which you will repeatedly ladle."

John Mallen, President, JMC Marketing Communications & PR

"I am so glad that yoga found Kathy and Dennis! The premise that *everything matters* puts life in perspective. Through their book and classes, they have taught the importance of breath and the connectedness of the physical, mental, and spiritual aspects of our lives. Their book gives a deeper understanding of the rich history of yoga and meditation and how impactful it can be on our health and lives. *Everything Matters* helps put life into perspective and creates more meaning to who we are and what we are about."

Joe Mitrick, Hospital President

"From the moment I met the Langs I felt a special connection and an energy that I couldn't really define at first. Over the years and as their journey has unfolded, it is clear that the energy is pure love. I can feel this come through in this book. Their love of life, of others, and most of all for one another shines brightly in each chapter. Their story and teachings in the book make the world a better place."

Linda H. Sherrer, Founder, President, and CEO of Berkshire Hathaway HomeServices Florida Network Realty

"What makes Dennis and Kathy Lang's work stand out is their inspired lyrical combination of styles and forms to achieve a harmonious and uplifting result. Their hearts flow through the work as their stories, instruments, and experiences feel like gifts that bring their students into a balanced sense of serenity."

Daniele Giovannucci, President, COSA
(Committee on Sustainability Assessment)

"If a yoga practice begins by rolling out a mat, a yogic life begins by opening *Everything Matters* by Dennis and Kathy Lang. In this book, they have peeled the onion for you. And in doing so, they achieve one of the book's primary goals: demystifying some of the principles of yoga. As a result, you will become intrigued by the depth of their warm, authentic approach. Your practice will change. Your outlook and the importance of your every action will purposefully magnify. In turn, everything around you, including the lives of those around you, will begin to shimmer and reflect the change in you. All of this, because— *Everything Matters.*"

Jill and Hal Mankin, yoga practitioners

TABLE OF CONTENTS

DEDICATION

With our deepest heartfelt thanks and gratitude, we dedicate this book to our families and to the teachers who inspired us.

In addition, we have the following special dedications to two beings who were instrumental in our transformation and are forever close to our hearts:

Ming, "The Wonder Dog," our canine teacher, the truly enlightened one. Human language falls short in describing the unconditional love we share as our three hearts merged as one. Her last lesson for us was, "Love each other and treat each other as I have loved and treated you; love like a dog would love—unconditionally." Ming forever lives on within us as the purest form of love and light. We will pay her love forward the rest of our lives.

Dr. Lori Tapp. Aside from being Dennis' cousin and a nationally recognized doctor of veterinary medicine, it was her most insightful comment years ago regarding current consciousness that was a major contribution and a source of inspiration for our transformation. For the whole story, go to the Reflection entitled, *The Question Became "Why."*

EVERYTHING MATTERS

Every moment is yours!

We are alive in the present—not yesterday, not tomorrow, but right now. Our bodies naturally know this, as our innate intelligence keeps us alive. In fact, our physiology is always present.

The same cannot be said for our psychology. We often live as though we are virtual time travelers, at least in the sense of our awareness. Really! We tend to live most of our awakened experience disconnected from the present. It's truly a paradox, as our bodies can only be in the present moment, but our minds can simultaneously be somewhere else.

Our life experiences are clouded with worries about the past and future. We are in constant states of stress due to career pressures, competition, achievement, acquisition, and consumption. Our hormonal mixes are as though we are being chased by a saber-toothed tiger rather than in serene balance with life as it flows. Correspondingly, our cortisol levels are not only higher but remain higher even into our sleeping hours. The world today is one of instantaneous communications, social media, and high-speed living. We are in a state of accelerated living.

During all this, our overall consciousness or awareness is not present and is therefore separated from our bodies. It's as though our state of being is one of a near-death, out-of-body experience, but while alive. Even though the body and brain system are directly linked physiologically and are present keeping us alive, this is not so for the body-*mind* system. In other words, the mind is out of touch with the body under these high-speed, high-stress conditions. The mind is not embodied.

This was an interesting realization for us, one among many we would learn along our path in yoga: to think that we can consciously exist outside of our bodies, truly be out-of-touch, living life in a mindless state of being.

Within these last paragraphs are several underlying messages and lessons learned from our yoga training, studies, and practices. Collectively these are the realizations that we are sharing in this book. But deeper within and common among all the realizations is one thread that holds true that was only recently revealed. We have peeled the onion to its core and found the central teaching that captures the essence of our life with yoga.

> *Kathy:* In the spring of 2016, a dear friend had asked us to join him as guest teachers for his program the following year at the Sivananda ashram in the Bahamas. The subject was "Food as a Spiritual Path." He had asked that we bring our perspective of yoga and meditative practices that would complement his message. Needless to say, we were honored.
>
> It was during the following months, as we developed our thoughts and content for our portion of the program, that this lesson was revealed. It came to Dennis during a deep meditation and became the theme of our presentation. That lesson is: "Everything matters!"

Everything matters. Every word you speak or think. Every thought, feeling, and emotion you have. Every breath you take. Every action, every reaction, and even your lack of action or reaction matters. It all matters greatly. Taking this simple phrase, *everything matters*, into our daily awareness brings importance to every moment. It reminds us that within each moment, all possibilities exist. How and what we do in each moment creates the propulsion into the next moment. And how and what we do, say, or even think affects those around us.

Our lives flow moment to moment, in the now, in the present—not in the past, not in the future. What's more, our lives here on earth are very, very limited, even if you live to be 108 years old. Time is too short. Yet we remain caught in the fog or in the tornado of life.

Our realization that everything matters is an acknowledgement that we were missing the point of life, the essence of our lives as individuals and as a couple. It reminds us that we make the choice in each moment of what our trajectory will be. We choose and define our reality. *Everything matters* also is a reminder that we are interconnected and interdependent, as our actions affect others and there is a ripple effect that spreads radially, touching all around us.

It's a responsibility to integrate this phrase into your life. It is not to be taken lightly. Knowing that everything we do matters places ownership where it belongs: with each of us. The incredible and amazing upside of this is that it's how each of us can truly make a difference in the world, because the how, what, when, and where of everything we do has an impact or leaves an impression on the world in some way, shape, or form, whether positively or negatively. When we remember that everything matters, we are empowered to take action—hopefully the right action—for the betterment of the world and all beings around us.

The first step to changing the world is changing yourself and knowing *everything matters.*

Namaste,
Dennis and Kathy Lang
Atlantic Beach, Florida
Summer 2018

OUR STORY

Who would have guessed that a husband and wife career couple, successfully climbing the corporate ladder, would now be full time yoga and meditation teachers? We certainly didn't—and none of our work associates, family, or friends did either! When we first met we were both young, driven for success, and ready to travel the world. There is no way we could have imagined completely reinventing our lifestyles.

Our lives as a couple began in 1982 when we both worked for the same company. For both of us, our meeting was something different from any other encounter in our lives and we knew it was bigger than us. It was simply right on all levels.

> *Dennis:* I knew immediately that Kathy was "the one." There was no hesitation or second thought, and no doubt. My gut reaction and my intuitive sense provided the clear and unquestionable knowing that we were meant to be together.
>
> In high school I had always wanted to date a cheerleader. I always admired them; aside from the obvious attractions, they are confident, hard workers, disciplined, and sincere, most of the time. Now, I was not a wallflower, but I was a bit of an introvert and somewhat of

a nerd. I was really into mathematics, electronics, and martial arts. In fact, my reputation with martial arts landed me the nickname "Grasshopper" in my high school year book.

While in college as an undergrad in engineering, my interest in mathematics grew exponentially (pun intended). The longer and more complex the math equation, the more I liked it. I finished my bachelor's degree and landed a full-boat research assistance position to continue my studies. My areas of focus were the mathematical modeling of sound transmission, biological cell division, and tree growth. Did I say I was a nerd?

I was on track to pursue a Ph.D. at Stanford University, but my MS thesis and its defense were so tough that I really needed a break to regroup. I thought that going out into industry to work for a year would add to my resume and blend some practical thought into my brain, so I took an engineering job based in Toledo. That's where I met Kathy. And here is the key point of this discussion: Be careful what you ask for! As it turns out, Kathy was co-captain of the cheerleading squad in high school and she lived on Stanford Avenue, so I got it all! The cheerleader from Stanford Avenue far outweighed a Ph.D. from Stanford University! We have been together ever since, over thirty-five years and still counting.

Kathy: Dennis didn't go into the detail of how we met. I had been at the company about six months when this new guy started, with a cubicle right next to mine. Of course I checked him out! This was a Monday. On Thursday we happened to be riding the elevator together. Being the southern girl I am, I thought I would be polite and introduce myself, so I did. He introduced himself back, the doors opened, and that was that.

The next day, Friday, I felt bad for the "new guy" and thought he probably didn't know anyone in town yet, so I invited him to happy hour with a bunch of us. I already had my eye on another guy and was just being friendly. Dennis said he would love to come but had taken the bus into work and didn't have his car. We both lived on the Southside of town, so I offered to give him a ride home—again, just being neighborly.

We go to happy hour, ready to unwind after a rough work week. I introduce Dennis to a few of my friends and then hunt down the guy I really want to talk to. I feel like I am making good progress when Dennis comes over and says he needs a ride home. It's only seven o'clock on a Friday night and I am pissed! I ask why he needs to leave so early, and he says he has a date at eight and needs to get back to his apartment to get ready. Seriously! Here I was feeling sorry for him because he didn't know anyone, he's been in town for a grand total of six days, and the dude has already met a girl and booked a date! Because I am always good for my word, I reluctantly left the happy hour and drove him home.

The next day, Dennis called to sort of apologize and asked what I was doing that night. I told him I was going to a party and, for some unknown reason, asked him if he wanted to tag along, not thinking that it was a date. We go to the party and spend hours talking until very late that night. The next day he moved in with me. Not in the sense of literally moving all his furniture, but in the sense that he brought over his toothbrush, shaving stuff, clothes, etc. So our story is that we met on a Thursday and he moved in on Sunday! Crazy, huh? Years later, Dennis told me that to a nerdy engineering student, when I introduced myself in the elevator, that was a pick-up line!

Now this might sound a little woo-woo, so get ready. Many healers and shamans have told us that we have been together many times in past lives so that's why it only took four days for us to come together in this life. We recognized each other right away on a subconscious level.

Psychoanalyst Carl Jung was the first to introduce the concept of synchronicity, the idea that events can occur with no causal or apparent relationship but in fact result in a meaningful relationship when later assessed. Our life together has been a living, breathing example of synchronicity. How else do a southern girl from Daytona Beach, Florida and a recent engineering grad from the backwoods of Erving, Massachusetts, end up working for the same company in Toledo, Ohio, with cubicles right next to each other, and fall in love in an elevator? Yes, synchronicity in action!

There would be many more examples of synchronicity as our journey together unfolded. We would later develop the ability to see and sense these occurrences. You see, as we became more aware and open through our yoga and meditation practices, our sensitivity to such occurrences improved. It's an ability that we can all develop. In our case it was not strategic as much as a by-product of our yogic practices.

• • •

With our corporate careers spanning over twenty years, we were very successful by many of society's standards. We were excellent at adapting within corporate cultures. In our professional roles we could see trends and read the business and internal political landscapes. We were competitive and would change career paths for advancement, ready, willing, and able to follow wherever our talents were needed. We really had it all: great jobs, lots of responsibility, world travel to more than thirty countries, big salaries, hefty bonuses, and excellent benefits. In other words, we were your classic corporate employees on the successful fast track—and yet, truth be told, something was lacking.

Over time, the hidden costs of our stressful careers began to emerge. Early signs manifested as short tempers, uncharacteristic reactions to situations, and weight fluctuations. Even with all of our education and hard work, we did not anticipate the costs associated with success. We began to wonder whether we could sustain and survive our success. After all, isn't it all about happiness, health, and longevity? We had all the trimmings and glitter of success, but our lights were dimming under the pressures of our corporate roles. What was the so-called end game for us?

> *Dennis*: I was so caught up in my job and corporate role that it became my identity: Dennis Lang, VP of this or that. It started to overtake me as an individual. My ego really got the best of me, a subtle but a potent affliction that I would later learn was an "attachment." In addition, there were corporate politics, which I managed to navigate and even excel at, but at the expense of others. I would lat-

er learn the concepts of karma, empathy, and compassion and became remorseful of some of my past tactics.

The other factor that wore on us was business travel. We both traveled a lot, but my travel became insane. My schedule looked like this: leave on a Monday and fly to Paris, come home Friday, leave forty-eight hours later and fly to Brazil for four days, come home for two days, then fly to Germany for six days. After years at this pace and intensity, something had to give.

It was not obvious at the time, but I had become a statistic, along with many others, of the impact of stress on the body-mind system. I was placed on blood pressure medication and diagnosed as pre-asthmatic, for which I was awarded drugs to be taken for the rest of my life. My weight drifted up, peaking at about forty-five pounds over my healthy weight. I was on a crash course, but oh was I successful!

Kathy was also very successful, but she had the ability to hold it in check. Watching her became a framed reference that grounded me as I grew more skeptical of my original corporate path. The issue of "surviving success" rose higher on my radar.

In retrospect, I fell into what is termed "the corporate tornado." The higher in the organization I climbed and the closer to the center I got, the larger my ego grew and the more powerful the drag on my being. I was blinded by my accomplishments and as new, higher responsibilities and authority were being placed upon me,

I was missing the most important aspects of life itself.

It was only after finding yoga that I wondered what true success actually was. Now, because of our reinvention—including major lifestyle and dietary changes—I am off all medications and have maintained my ideal weight for the last fifteen years.

YOGA FOUND US, AKA WE DID NOT SEE THIS COMING!

Yoga found us, as we like to say. We were not seeking it out. In fact, it was not on our radar at all, or even in our consciousness. In 2000, while vacationing at a resort, yoga was just an option on the daily activities list. With no real thought we said, "Why not give it a shot?" Little did we know that this would be the beginning of a monumental change in direction for us.

Dennis: I thought yoga would be a meditative and strange experience, very "woo woo" if you will. My left brain, corporate-driven male mind was ready to go "do" this yoga class. Little did I know that it would "do" me in terms of leaving a permanent, positive impression, like an energetic tattoo.

Kathy: At the time, we were long distance runners. We didn't have any friends who were doing yoga and we knew nothing about it except we thought it might be a good stretching class to help our running. The instructor was very sweet and I remember watching some of the other students easily getting into these crazy poses. Of course, both of us being competitive types, we tried to do the same with force and vigor, which only resulted in sore muscles

for days. We had anticipated an easy class of simple movements but, looking back, it was exactly what we needed at
the time—a challenging class that fed our egos. That was
what got us interested in learning more.

We had assumed that all yoga was the same—really New Age, meditative, and weird. As it turned out, we had stumbled into the infamous
Ashtanga primary series as our very first yoga experience. Whoa and
wow all at once! It blew us away and shifted our ideas of what yoga
was. The Ashtanga primary series is a very physical and dynamic practice with integrated breathing and controlled transitions in and out of
amazing poses. It was the perfect first experience for us as it left a strong
impression and was so contrary to our misconceptions.

You see, had this been a gentle yoga class it would not have left such a
strong impression. We were both so in our heads, especially Dennis with
his male ego and competitive drive, that this very physically challenging
practice kind of set him in his place. The practice met us right where we
were in our lives and infused a taste of something more. No other so-
called fitness experience had ever stayed with us like this first yoga class.
It really touched us both, and we would speak of this class for years to
come. Of course, as we now know, it really was much more than a fitness
class, but at the time we did not have the insight to understand.

After this first class, we eased our way into a steady practice of yoga over
the next couple of years. We found a local studio with weekly classes and
became regulars. We even hired the teacher, Kate, for a private lesson to
explain alignment and some of the strange concepts (at the time) like
Mula Bandha and chakras.

For us, transformation came gradually. The yoga mat became a mirror
reflecting our true selves as we began to observe, investigate, and inquire.

It was not just about our alignment within a posture but also our energetic alignment, the alignment of our relationships with ourselves, each other, and the world around us. The postures and sequences became metaphors of our lives, within which we expressed ourselves and met ourselves as we were in the moment.

As we kept practicing and studying, our desire for the next class or workshop felt as strong as our need for food. The more we practiced, the more we noticed subtle changes. We were relaxing and releasing the stresses of our physical, mental, and energetic selves. We saw ourselves as individuals, us as a couple, and the world around us through a different lens. Life started to become clearer. We began to see trends in our lifestyle. The process of self-examination became an ongoing practice, on and off the mat. We began to realize that while we were thriving in our corporate lives, running parallel was an ever-growing negative energy that was beginning to take hold. Our connection to our inner truth had become incompatible with our lifestyle, so much so that we could feel it physically as an illness felt in the gut.

Although our careers provided and supported our lifestyle, it was at the high expense of our health and happiness. In fact, if something did not give, we were destined to hit a wall of some sort and it would not end well. We were thriving and surviving, but not really living—by that we mean not living holistically in balance, not living in alignment with our inner essence, and not living in harmony with nature or the universe. As we were developing and growing in our yoga practices, we often would catch ourselves thinking and saying that we are human "beings," not human "doings"!

YES, we are Beings, not Doings. We shifted our awareness and our actions toward "living and being." It was this realization that became the genesis of the reinvention and transformation of ourselves and us as a couple.

Kathy: One day I asked Dennis, "Would you continue your career if it were not for the money?" First observing and then being truthful in his response, he said no. That moment was the beginning of our re-direction.

Dennis: That question hit me hard. It struck a chord, a dissonant chord. Kathy's timing was perfect as I had been practicing yoga long enough and had studied enough to know that honesty with yourself and others was a key learning of yoga. This comes from the Yoga Sutras and is known as Satya, which in Sanskrit means *truthfulness*.

Another result of yoga practice is the ability to listen, ingest, digest, and allow for the inner wisdom to express itself and provide guidance. I knew the answer deep inside. It became clear that we had arrived at another turning point in our lives. Our corporate careers had served us well, but now was a new day.

Our lifestyle had to change. We had no choice. Physically, mentally, emotionally, and energetically we had to change trajectory. All the money and perks of our jobs were no longer meaningful or feeding us spiritually.

Yoga provided the framework to notice, observe, and inquire within as well as the methodology to discern and assess the reality of the situation. And truthfulness, satya, is a must as well. We as a species are so good at telling ourselves stories and not acknowledging the truth. For many of us, this delusional dialog with ourselves is the main cause of our issues.

Our realization culminated in the need for a complete make-over, all pointing toward our ultimate goal to be full-time yoga and meditation teachers. We had benefited so much from yoga and meditation that we wanted to share our learning and experiences with all who would listen.

Now, this is all easier said than done! This change required leaving the comfort zone, pushing our edges, stepping into the unknown and leaning into discomfort. As we like to say in our yoga classes, the transitions are just as important as the pose itself. So it is in life. Adjusting your course in life, and certainly reinventing yourself, are transitions that require attention and awareness so that your arrival into the next pose/career/location/lifestyle is safe, secure, and sustainable.

In 2005, we completed our initial yoga teacher training and soon thereafter we both resigned from our corporate positions on the same day in August.

> *Kathy*: It took a lot of faith. We went from being really valued employees to unknowns! Quite a jump!
>
> After I submitted my resignation from the big corporate job, it was interesting to see the reactions from co-workers. One by one, they would come into my office, close the door and give me one of two reactions. Half of them said, *Are you nuts? You have a great job with a high salary and benefits, and the company spent a lot of money on your training!* But the other half said, *I wish I had your guts to walk out of this place. If only I didn't have the _____ (fill in the blank here: mortgage, kids in college, credit card debt, etc.), I'd do the same thing.*
>
> *Dennis*: Of course, my boss thought I was making a power play and that I had turned in my resignation just to squeeze him for more money or a bigger job. He offered me several other positions, all with increased responsibil-

ity, higher salary, and more employees reporting to me. But that was not at all what I was looking for. It took two weeks of me rejecting these options before he realized that I was serious about leaving the company.

We certainly did not see this coming. How yoga could become such a part of our lives was unexpected. How this happened and how it works is the bottom line of this book. It's the magic of yoga that lies below the surface. Yoga became as much a part of us as the blood flowing through our veins. It became the food that nourished us and the energy that sustained us. Yoga became our navigation system guiding us though life, always keeping our awareness grounded and in alignment with our true north.

Our approach was methodical and logical. We did not simply decide to drop out, quit our jobs, and go live in a yurt. We assessed and adjusted our finances accordingly to allow for the transition between our corporate careers and becoming full-time yoga teachers. We needed some type of work to bridge the gap while we honed our teaching skills, added more training and practice, and developed our personal brand, so we decided to become real estate agents.

For those of you who know real estate, it's a flexible career path—until you are successful, that is. Then it OWNS you! Not surprisingly, we brought our same corporate-driven mentality into our "transition job" of real estate. After building a strong network of clients, we found ourselves becoming top producers. This career, which was only supposed to be a "bridge," activated old triggers from our corporate past that caused the same stressors. However, this time around we had the tools provided by our yoga and meditation training to observe, assess, and adjust. We quit real estate, handed our business over to a friend, and stepped onto the full-time yoga-teaching path. We have not looked back since.

WHY THIS BOOK

"Wherever you go, there you are."
— *Jon Kabat-Zinn*

This quote is such an obvious statement, both concise and profound. For the first forty-plus years of our lives, we had not realized this fundamental truth as so eloquently stated by Jon Kabat-Zinn, creator of the Stress Reduction Clinic and the Center for Mindfulness in Medicine, Health Care, and Society at the University of Massachusetts Medical School. It's *so* true. Upon reflection of our lives and travels together, we realized that our minds were always there. No matter where we were, for better or worse, positively or negatively our minds—and therefore our thoughts, feelings and emotions—were always with us. It seems so obvious now!

Awareness of thoughts and our relationship to them was not a part of our consciousness, and yet we were certainly *conscious*—at least to some degree. We did not understand how awareness was connected to consciousness, health, or the body-mind system itself. How was it that we could function in very successful corporate jobs, travel the world, live an amazing life together, and miss something so obvious?

It took years of yogic study and practice for us to unravel this mystery for ourselves. In doing so, we shifted our consciousness toward a new path that was so different, it seemed unreal and even strange at times.

Along the way, it certainly was not easy. We learned to observe ourselves and our lives with a new perspective. Observations led to inquiry and assessment, which in turn led to response. "Wherever you go, there you are," became foundational to our life experience and a thread, almost mantra-like, as we wove a new tapestry for our lives.

Our new journey was initiated back in 2000 when we took our first yoga class. At the time we had no idea that a seed had been planted in both of us that would lead to literally re-inventing ourselves. This was the first step on a new path toward self-realization and the transformation of us as a couple. They say, "When the student is ready, the teacher will appear." In our case, it was the teacher of that first yoga class, which led to our meeting the ultimate teacher—the guru within each of us—who would emerge later after many yoga practices, workshops, and trainings.

So why a book? It's a question that we wrestled with for many years.

Actually, several questions kept haunting us. First of all, do we have anything relevant to say? What among our experiences are so interesting to justify a book? Does the world need another book on self-help, yoga, realization, or transformation? Have we learned anything over the last seventeen years that we can convey in a meaningful way to help others? Would a book by us be a positive influence and have an impact on the world around us?

Aside from our own growing interest in taking on this writing project, various friends, healers, teachers, and students would occasionally bring up the idea. It seemed that, as our teaching and workshops expanded and we were connecting with more people, there was an interest in us that emerged in others. This interest revolved around how we were able to so dramatically re-invent ourselves both individually and also in unison as a couple, and still remain in a loving, happy partnership after this transformation. How do two people such as us survive an in-depth renovation and re-design as individuals and as a couple?

These inquiries even opened *our* eyes as we wondered and reflected upon ourselves as to how we arrived here. Did we simply drink the proverbial cool-aid? What was the process? What were the elements, forces, and energies that came together that led us down this path? How did we transform from having very successful corporate careers to being a yoga teaching couple, and how did we do it together, hold it together, and survive it together?

One of the great lessons of yoga and meditation is to be both the "observer" and the "observed" during practice. When we are able to do this, we connect deeply within and can then assess our mental terrains, emotions, thoughts, feelings, patterns, etc. Observation leads to understanding, which in turn leads to awareness. Awareness must, however, come from a place of nonjudgmental truthfulness. It was this awareness, learned through yoga, that caused us to notice variances between the path we were on and the path of our true selves. The paths of our true selves were miraculously unified together in our love for each other.

In retrospect, there emerged key reflections which were the by-products of our practices over the years. These became the platform of the process that molded and re-directed us. This overall understanding seemed to bubble up as boiling water creates steam, or in this case, emerged as the subject matter for this book. We are not sure which came first, the interest expressed by others in our story, or the internal desire to take on such a project with the hope it might help others find their way. In any event, it's as though we were guided to do so.

Having decided to step into the cold waters of publishing our story and the seemingly daunting task of writing a book, we do so humbly. In the spirit of the Yoga Sutras, which we will discuss in more detail as they relate to our lives, this book is an authentic offering of our truth as found through the study and practice of yoga and meditation. Our hope is that there might be just some small nugget of knowledge or speck of wisdom that we have gained that might shed a light on darkness for others. As we say in our workshops and classes, we are just conduits and guides. Yes, we are very well trained and highly credentialed, with many hours of teaching experience, but we are students first and we see our teachers everywhere and in everyone. Our learning is a continuous and lifelong process.

We refer to ourselves as "traditional non-traditionalists" or "non-denominational yogis" in that we honor all traditions and styles of yoga. By choice and by design, we do not follow any one tradition and we are non-dogmatic in our views and practices. It's an authentic approach for us as we naturally love all of life and feel there are many paths to the summit.

Any knowledge or wisdom that we have gained through yoga, meditation, or mindfulness is not ours to hold. It's all to be shared for the benefit of others. We are facilitators and guides of an experience that may lead to self-realization, and hopefully leave the world a better place than when we arrived.

If you bought this book, we are thankful and grateful for your conscious choice to spend time with us through this medium. A poem, letter, article, or book takes the reader into the mind's eye or consciousness of the writer at the time of publication. While we were not able to resolve all of our own questions listed above about writing a book, we still felt guided to do so—guided as though we are directed by a force bigger than ourselves to use this medium as a means of expression to capture the teachings, reflections, and practices we have learned up to this point in our journey. As with many things in life, one must just go with the flow and not always know why. In fact, we find the more we let go, the more in the flow we are. Such is the case with this project.

There is an ocean of books published on yoga, meditation, and mindfulness. Our purpose herein is to make our presentation concise, clear, and meaningful for everyday use. We do not want this to read as a dissertation on the subject, but as an authentic expression of our learning and experience. Although we are not medical doctors, psychologists, psychotherapists, or nutritionists, we will touch upon each of these areas as it relates to our own experiences and practices from a holistic perspective of health, happiness, and wellness. In addition, we want to demystify some of the principles of yoga and meditation that we feel have become overcomplicated relative to the ancient texts or have drifted off course, at least according to us. We believe we as a culture tend to make life far more complicated than it needs to be and that we live life too fast.

The teachings of yoga are for the most part relatively simple and straightforward, but are not easy to put into practice. The good news is that, over time, practicing consistently brings yoga *into* you, and then the magic of yoga begins. You see, part of the magic is that you do not "do" yoga, you *be* yoga.

This work is a view inside our authentic selves. It is an outward expression of our belief that we all make a difference and have a meaningful impact on the world around us. This book, our teaching, music, and meditations are collectively an expression of our love for each other and for the world around us. It is our sincere hope that this work is useful in a positive way, to lift up the present moment for you, and that our actions are for the benefit of all beings.

Upon reflection, Everything Matters!

HOW TO USE THIS BOOK

We organized this book to match how our experiences, practice, and training led to our own transformation. Throughout the book, we will include individual commentaries by each of us as we each have personal thoughts in addition to our blended views as a couple.

Everything Matters is the overarching lesson. After all our years of study, practice, travels, and teaching, this key truth was revealed recently during a meditation. So profound was this that it is now part of our everyday consciousness.

In **Our Story,** we tell a little about us and summarize our first exposure and impressions that lead into our deeper journey on the yogic path.

Foundations of Yoga offers a different way of looking at yoga based on ancient foundations including how to harness the power of the mind, balance and open the energetic channels of the body, improve your relationships with yourself and others, and understand how the history of this ancient practice plays into a modern-day approach.

Next are the **Practices** themselves. Here is where you'll

find the actual *things you can do,* including an overview of what practice actually is, how to incorporate meditation and mindfulness in a busy life, tips on starting and maintaining a physical practice at home, and living as practice.

The **Reflections** section presents key nuggets we derived from our years of practicing and teaching. Think of these as the key takeaways (to use our former corporate jargon!) that we consider to be essential learnings that shaped and directed us toward transformation. These include thoughts on how to stay on the path, how to follow your dharma as a practice for the betterment of those around you and society at large, and how to share the path as a couple. Each Reflection reads like a short essay; a great way to use this section is to randomly choose one and read it as a stand-alone.

The **Appendices** provide a summary of our favorite mantras and several meditations from our published collections. These can be helpful as you might develop your own personal practice.

FOUNDATIONS
OF YOGA

YOGA: IT'S NOT WHAT YOU THINK

To paraphrase Einstein, "The more we know, the less we know."

Yoga is India's greatest gift to the world and we are indebted recipients of that gift! We are humbled by the history and tradition of yoga. In this book and in our lives, we are standing upon the shoulders of all who have gone before us. We are often reminded as we stand in Tadasana, a foundational pose in yoga, to reflect upon the millions over the millennia who have taken that shape as a pose of honor and initiation of Surya Namaskar (Sun Salutation). Therefore, we are passionate about preserving the traditions and history of yoga, especially here in the US which seems to focus so heavily on the physical practice.

Yoga is an art, one that cuts across all aspects of human experience. It's also an empirical science and technology that requires practice. Rubber meets the road on the mat. With its various traditions, studies, practices, and rituals, yoga touches upon physiology, psychology, psychotherapy, anatomy, therapeutics, energetics, astrology, sound, vibration, music, spirituality, sustainability, health, happiness, wellness, and longevity. Whew! That's a long list! Needless to say, it's both an extremely broad and very deep subject. Certainly it's not just a "30 days to a new you" kind of program, although that's a good start. This is not to diminish the body's importance as part of the self-realization mix. In fact, our bodies are integral to our growth in yoga, as they are our most tangible asset, and although there has been a dilution of the history and tradition of yoga here in the US, the true essence of yoga still flourishes and surfaces even in the most powerful of power vinyasa studios.

Most yoga studios, at least in the US, emphasize the physical side of yoga as that has proven over the past decade to be the most commercially viable approach. Also, it's the hook that gets most of us interested. Like the majority of us, our first exposure to yoga was on the physical level, and it's natural in our culture to be drawn to the physical. Yes, you can stay on the surface and get a great workout with all the physical benefits of asana (postures), but that's just skimming across the surface when there is so much more!

> *Kathy*: Yoga has been so diluted in the US and many other western cultures that it's like drinking an Orange Crush and thinking that's what a real orange must taste like. I remember we were at a big yoga conference early on in our yoga exploration, and I overheard a young yoga student say to her friend, "Well, you know, yoga was invented in California." Can you imagine my shock and horror at this statement! Yes, the first yoga *studio* in the US was opened in Hollywood, CA by a Russian actress, Indra Devi, in 1946. She taught yoga to the likes

of Greta Garbo, Eva Gabor, and Gloria Swanson. Indra was a true trendsetter and on the leading edge of a wave that would later crest in the mid-60s and explode into a multi-billion-dollar industry in the 21st century. But, my friends, yoga was not invented in California.

We've strayed so far from the source that many yogis don't even know its history! It's almost by definition that yoga seeks more of us than just a workout. Whereas a workout is a physical regime to improve one's fitness or enhance athletic performance, yoga is not—although it *will* certainly enhance athletic or competitive performance as an integral cross-training method. There is no expectation, no judgement, no comparison, and no goals in the practice of yoga per se. Without comparison, expectation, judgement, and goals, what would a workout be?

To tap into the real benefits of yoga, it helps to be willing and open to exploring these depths. Once you are, you'll find that it's the "work-in" rather than the "workout" where yoga really happens. In other words, yoga will meet you where you are and deliver what you seek.

ANCIENT PHILOSOPHIES
FOR CURRENT TIMES

One fascinating aspect of yoga is its long history and tradition. If so many before us, generation after generation, have been practicing this ancient art and science, there must be something right about these philosophies and practices. Like so many yogis who have gone before us, we have been drawn in and inspired by this. In our years studying yoga philosophically, psychologically, and physically, what we found was far more rich than simple calisthenics passed on over the years since the word "yoga" was first coined. We quickly realized yoga is about so much more and these ancient teachings apply in today's world just as they did long ago. What incredible insight the ancient sages and masters had about the human condition!

As we sit here in now in northeast Florida co-creating this book, we look back upon our many travels, domestic and foreign, and we look across the general populations with so many economic and technological advancements, and yet there is so much suffering. We live in a time in which, collectively, we can create and destroy our world time and time again. Incredible, seemingly unlimited resources are available to provide happy and healthy lives for all inhabitants. We are living in a world of amazing advancements on all fronts. Yet so many are unhappy and suffering. How is this the case? Is this unique to this time in history?

Civilization as we know it is more than 6,000 years old. Although some estimate that humans—as in Homo Sapiens—have existed for more than 200,000 years (Harari, 2015), it took a very long time for humans to coalesce into tribes and form organized communities. It was not until much later, in the 1800s, that the industrialization that accelerated growth and development across major regions of the world began. To put this growth into perspective, the world population was 170 million in 1 CE (worldpopulationhistory.org), about 970 million in 1800, and now exceeds 7.5 billion. That means it took 1800 years—from year 1 to year 1800—for the population to grow 5.7 times bigger than it was, and then just over 200 years after the Industrial Revolution—from 1800 to now—for it grow by a factor of 7.8! Our world population has exploded!

It's easy to think that, with all our technological advances, our lives would become more balanced and we would be happier. But we aren't.

> *Dennis*: I remember watching a *60 Minutes* segment about thirty years ago which presented a futuristic view of how information technology would shift our lives over the next twenty years. Here we are now, ten years beyond the projection, and I must say there have been many advancements in communications, travel, distribution systems, and countless other ways in which technology has pushed humanity along. Yet, with it all, stress, obesity, cancer, suicides, and countless other manifestations of ill-health and sadness have grown exponentially. With all of our progress, we are less happy and less balanced in many ways than our ancestors.

Regardless of size and advancements, the greatest civilizations of the past shared a common element with us today: the human element. Evolution is a very slow process; as humans we are basically the same today as we were several thousand years ago. Infrastructure, agriculture, commerce, and culture have changed and coalesced, creating lifestyles for each population in each era. Over our collective history, civilizations come and go. Some expand; some contract or meet eventual demise. But however successful, challenged, or defunct, the one common element amongst all civilizations is that we are still human. All that's changed is the nature of our lifestyles vis-á-vis technology.

Back in the days of the first yogis, 5,000 years ago, some sages and other enlightened ones made the same observations about their civilization: that even with all the advancements, people were not happy. Villages had developed exchange, trade, agriculture, government, and society to support the collective and yet there was something lacking in culture—perhaps something similar to what we lack today—that motivated these ancient seers to observe with a different view. They might have asked, how can it be that so many live in discontent? With all the developments of the day, how can these souls be so unhappy?

Perhaps it was this line of thinking that led some to consider the question and develop philosophies and practices for the benefit of humanity. These deep thinkers found refuge in the forests, removing themselves from the sensory input of the villages so that they could receive insights.

What they observed and learned in these early days is evident in their writings for our benefit today. Our happiness is up to us. It's all in our heads. It's all in our minds. In these ancient texts, the use of meditation, mantra practices, and the power of repetition is presented not just as a form of affirmation, but as a means to manage and develop the mind. Interestingly, very little is presented and mentioned about asana, the physical postures.

TODAY, AS IT WAS IN ANCIENT TIMES, IT'S ALL ABOUT THE MIND

Physiologically, psychologically, and, we might add, energetically, humans today are essentially the same as back in the ancient times. People then and now are faced with the same issues and afflictions, but the root causes or triggers of today are perhaps advanced due to technology.

The world today needs to remember these great teachings. It seems we are more and more caught up in the vortex of our fast lives, that we forget these many lessons from this great period in history. We are all sentient beings, we all want happiness, and yet so many are not happy at all. It's truly paradoxical how we have such amazing technological advancement, and yet we make life so complex.

The real truth is, life is simple; it's about present moment awareness.

A LITTLE PERSPECTIVE ON THE HISTORY OF YOGA: IT WASN'T INVENTED HERE

With respect to yoga, history has shown the early traces of civilization dating at least back to 3000 BCE. This was a time of transition as the Indus Valley of India civilizations collapsed, leading to the emergence of the Vedic era that started about 1200 BCE. More than 3,000 years ago, populations were small and centralized into villages that recognized the advantage of community agriculture, commerce, and trade, although it was primitive by our scale. It was back then, at the forefront of civilization, that yoga emerged.

It was not until almost 5,000 years later, in 1893 in Chicago at the Parliament of World Religions, that Swami Vivekananda introduced yoga to America. This means that yoga came to America only *after* several millennia of existence.

The foundations of yoga are uncovered in the early sacred texts of the Vedic and pre-classical periods of yoga (Feuerstein, 2003). From the Vedic period, about 5,000 years ago, came the *Vedas*. The *Rig Veda* is said to be the oldest and perhaps the most ancient of writings in human history. The Vedas were heard—downloaded, if you will—by sages during deep meditations. They are a collection of teachings of life, rituals, practices, and praise hymns for spiritual development. A mantra that is important to us, the Gayatri Mantra (Rig Veda, Mandala 3.62.10), is believed to be one of the most ancient mantras in human history and was first recorded here.

The *Upanishads*, also referred to as the *Vedanta* or the last chapters of the *Vedas*, are among the most important literature in Indian history and culture. There are said to be more than 200 texts that are the highest wisdom of the Vedas. The Upanishads were written by multiple authors, likely forest dwellers, over a very long period ranging from about 800 BC to 300 BC and are extremely foundational in the history and evolution of yoga. They provide insights into the spiritual foundation and introduce the very definition of yoga, the concepts of energetic anatomy and prana (life force), and the importance of meditation and mantra chanting. In fact, the Katha Upanishad (c. 500-400 BC) emphasizes that self-realization is achieved through meditation. The Maitri Upanishad (c.300 BC) presented a six-fold path to oneness about 700 years before the eight-fold path of the Yoga Sutras of Patanjali, a foundation of current yoga that is discussed below.

Another of the most sacred and revered texts of yoga is found in the Upanishads as part of the world's most epic poem, the *Mahabharata*. We refer here to the *Bhagavad Gita* (we like the translation by Mitchell, 2000). The Gita, as it is commonly known, is the story of a young warrior who learns about life, dharma, duty, and yoga from his teacher, Krishna. The Gita is a pillar among all the texts of yoga and its teachings go beyond yoga. It's absolutely poetic in some ways. Every teacher of yoga should read at least one translation of the Gita.

THE YOGA SUTRAS

Perhaps the most referenced ancient manuscript on yoga is the Yoga Sutras of Patanjali (Bryant, 2009). Sutras can be thought of like sutures, or threads, that tie the concepts of yoga together. Organized as a series of bullet points—aphorisms, really—and arranged into four chapters, the Yoga Sutras codified yoga. It is perhaps the most translated, interpreted, and key cornerstone text written in the history of yoga. As with the Gita, every yoga teacher should read at least one translation (and preferably three) to really get a reasonable understanding of this incredible text. The Sutras very concisely lay out the art of consciousness and how to manage and guide the mind towards samadhi, or bliss. Consider it the user's guide to self-realization.

Our purpose herein is not to provide an in-depth analysis of the sutras, as there are many more qualified writers and scholars who have done so (and we are fans). However, a brief look at the Sutras and what it contains is important to understand yoga.

The Sutras consist of four chapters. They are:

1. **Samadhi Pada**: Introduces yoga and discusses the mind and its afflictions. This chapter very methodically presents the nature of our minds and how internal and external stimuli and thoughts affect us.

2. **Sadhana Pada**: Defines the path and practices of yoga. Here the eight limbs, or branches, of yoga are presented as an integrated means to quiet the chatter of the mind. Continuous practice over a long period is emphasized. Among the eight limbs, only one addresses the physical aspects, the asana or postures, of practice. However, no postures or sequences are specified, only the *qualities* achieved in a proper pose.

3. **Vibhuti Pada**: Exceptional powers are reviewed, which are a result of long-term practice. A very exciting chapter! Want a super power? Check out this chapter!

4. **Kaivalya Pada:** Liberation is presented as a final benefit of long-term practice. Samadhi, nirvana, or enlightenment: Call it what you will, this is the state of peace, joy, and happiness.

The eight limbs listed in Sadhana Pada, Chapter Two—sometimes called the eight-fold path—are a main foundation of yoga.

- The first two limbs, the yamas and niyamas, relate to how we interact with the world and how we observe and manage ourselves.
- The third limb, asana, refers to physical yoga.
- The forth limb, pranayama, addresses energy or prana and how to extend and expand it.
- The fifth, pratyahara, deals with the five senses.
- The final three limbs—dharana, dhyana, and samadhi—represent a progression from concentration to meditation and, finally, to bliss.

These eight limbs are not necessarily meant to be followed in a stepwise manner, and some of the steps will take most of us mere mortals the rest of our lifetimes, if accomplished at all. This is not surprising when you consider that the goal of the Sutras is self-realization. Notice what a tiny part of this eight-fold path has to do with a physical yoga practice! That is how small a part of yoga the physical poses actually are.

HERE IS A BRIEF SUMMARY
OF EACH OF THE EIGHT LIMBS:

1: Yamas
Restraints to follow, social discipline
- Ahimsa - non-harming, non-violence
- Satya - truthfulness
- Asteya - non-covetousness, non-greediness
- Bramacharya - conservation of energy and right action
- Aparigraha - non-possessiveness, non-attachment

2: Niyamas
Observances, individual discipline
- Saucha - purity and cleanliness
- Santosha - contentment
- Tapas - austerity, practice, self-discipline
- Svadhyaya – self-study
- Ishvara Pranidhana - devotion, we are part of something larger

3: Asana
Physical practice with the right intention, attention, and awareness

4: Pranayama
Breath management and manipulation to enhance the prana within

5: Pratyhara
Removal of the senses to deepen the connection to presence

6: Dharana
Concentration

7: Dhyana
Meditation

8: Samadhi
State of oneness

THE SUTRAS BECOME THREADS
FOR LIFE OFF THE MAT

We are not our bodies, but our bodies are a gateway toward this goal of self-realization. To achieve this requires us to meet the truth within us through contemplative practices. Yoga, like some other movement traditions such as Qi Gong and Tai Chi, utilizes the body as the means to connect to the present moment.

The Sutras remind us that it's the chatter and disturbances of our minds that get in the way of presence, and that it's via mindful awareness—with right action and practices—that we can reconnect to presence. Over time, with repeated practice, we learn to manage the chatter and calm the mind, allowing for balanced and harmonious existence.

As serious students of yoga, our experience has revealed that we must practice and consider the Yoga Sutras both on and off the mat. We learned over the years to extend our practice into our lifestyle, and that it's not enough to just practice yoga asana on the mat if your intention is larger than getting a good workout. For example, the first two limbs, the yamas and niyamas, are principles that are not limited to practicing on the mat. They are useful in everyday life.

Now, this was not revealed to us through intense meditation in a cave in Tibet. It's a realization through our own personal experiences from long-term practice. And this is a key reflection that has shaped and guided us on our path of yoga.

IT TAKES ALLOWANCE AND WILLINGNESS

Yoga will meet you where you are and provide you with what you seek. How we practice and how we apply it is up to us. Each day we come to the mat, we arrive as we are whether we know it or not!

The "know it or not" part refers to our awareness, the degree to which we are truly present and connected with experiencing the practice and experiencing our lives. As in everything we do, the quality and nature of our arrival is key to our experience.

To tap into the deeper aspects of yoga and reveal the nature of our relationships, we must have an interest to go there. Interest leads to willingness, followed by allowance—meaning that we allow the practice to work on us. To delve deeper into the practice, we have to consciously choose to do so. This means we have to be open to more than just a workout.

If you are willing and open yourself up, your essence will be revealed through yoga. It is possible to practice yoga just on the surface, but this would be such a limited experience, a series of calisthenics when really yoga is a "work-in."

> *Dennis:* This is where I was in the beginning. I saw yoga as just a nice way to stretch, and as a good cross-training for my long-distance running. There was no awareness of yoga relative to relationships on any level. I did not know what I did not know.
>
> I would say the keys to a deeper yoga experience and practice are an open mind, willingness to learn something new, allowance, and listening to what arrives and is revealed through the practice. There is a part of me which always was open-minded, and it was this slight crack in the door of my consciousness that allowed yoga to enter.
>
> *Kathy:* When students come up to us after one of our yoga classes and say, "Wow, that was a great workout,"

I am almost offended at first because I feel like I didn't do my job by taking them below the physical practice into a deeper place. But then I smile at that person and realize that they are me! I was the one early on looking for the great workout. I was the one who had not realized yet that yoga was not about the strong movements or the pretzel poses. So if someone thinks they are purely rolling out their mat for a workout, just give them time, and hopefully yoga will work its magic on them.

YOGA IS ABOUT RELATIONSHIPS

It took us a long while to make the connection between what the Sutras were about and what we thought we were doing on our mats. We realized that the Yoga Sutras are essentially about relationships—*all* our relationships. In the context of yoga, we use "relationship" to mean a mindful practice with right intention. So the practice becomes an examination of our relationship with ourselves, with others, with the world, and with spirit.

To be alive is to be in relationship continuously; flowing with each moment, we must live with the fullest of awareness and right intentions or desires. This is not a new concept—just look to the Upanishads:

> *You are what your deep, driving desire is. As your will is,*
> *so is your deed. As your deed is, so is your destiny.*
> — *Brihadaranyaka Upanishad*

Living in this embodied existence, in the interaction of our body-mind-spirit system with the world and the universe, is fundamental to our growth as human beings. It is through our relationships that we connect to all aspects of our lives and our interactions with all that surround us. That is to say, every single part of our existence is interconnected to and interacting with all that surrounds us.

Within every moment, we are relating. Within the space between stimulus and response there is the gap in which we choose how the next moment will be. This is the practice of life. Our relationships are all-encompassing and completely ours to manage as we create our own life experiences. For better or worse, we each choose.

The relationships of yoga are:

1. You with Yourself

Yourself means all aspects of self, including the physical, mental, emotional, and energetic layers. Your relationship with yourself is really the starting place on the path to realization. For example, the more asana we practice with mindful intention, the more we develop deeper insight into the nature of ourselves. Perhaps it begins with our weight. Holding crescent warrior pose with prayer twist is just one of many poses that will help you feel your girth and facilitate a desire to lose a couple of pounds.

Whether it's a concern about weight loss, substance abuse, past traumas, or stress reduction, the underlying issues lie within. The Yoga Sutras take our inner relationships deeper via the Niyamas, the second of the eight limbs. We must learn more about ourselves within the framework of the Niyamas in order for our true nature to be revealed.

The five Niyamas, observances of ourselves, are purity, contentment, austerity, self-study, and surrender. Of the five, we have found self-study, Svadhyaya, to be the means by which we first notice our own true divine nature. From this awareness we become our own witness, and the other four Niyamas follow as we evaluate, adapt, and change our habits and actions.

This is an inside-out process. Ideally it does require an open, mindfully aware, and willing approach to the practice. However, even for those who practice just for a workout, these deeper effects will likely make themselves known over time.

Yoga is about purification: On the surface we feel it through breath and respiration. Deeper within we feel it through emotional intelligence.

2. You with Others

As our time with the practice grows, we become aware of our interactions with those around us. Specifically, we are referring to our family, friends, and work associates, our sphere of influence. How we navigate each day, how our attitude, energies, and intensities affect those around us, becomes more visible. We become more sensitive to how our actions, words, and thoughts are received.

An example might be taking yourself too seriously, as though the world revolves around you. Like, it's all about you! It is our nature to want to control our environment and influence the world around us. We all want it our way. But that's a bit arrogant if you consider there are over seven billion people on the planet and they all want it their way as well! This need to control sends an aggressive, negative energy out to your sphere of influence.

As we bring this energy to the mat, our yoga practice becomes a metaphor (and the mat a mirror) of our negative energies. We express negative energy in our practices by how we transition into and out of a pose, how we express or even force a pose. It's all there on the mat. The more we practice, the more these rough edges soften and the more we become aware of these tendencies.

The first limb of the eight limbs of the Yoga Sutras, the Yamas, address this tendency and other social interactions very well. Of all of them, the first Yama, ahimsa, non-violence, is the key entry to the others.

Ahimsa is typically assumed to mean *non-violence upon others*. Sort of like, thou shalt not kill. But it runs deeper in the yogic context. Ahimsa also means non-harming in thought, word, action, and deed toward all beings, including yourself. It must be wicked important, as Patanjali lists it first among the eight limbs!

Violence can be explicit or implied; it can be obvious or energetic. Although we may not have intentions to physically bring harm to someone, most of us have had our share of negative thoughts toward others. Even negative thoughts are examples of violence. To have harmful thoughts and to harbor and obsess over them brings violence within yourself, and this negative energy is radiated outward and manifests as negative attitudes toward others.

Jealousy, envy, judgement, and criticism are a few examples of negative thoughts which, even if held privately in our own minds, can be radiated toward others. Observing our violent tendencies, even the most superficial, might be quite surprising.

We operate in auto-pilot mode most of the time, with little awareness. Taking just a moment to step back, pause, and notice any sort of negative or violent thoughts we have might just be an eye opener. The pause could save us from pulling the trigger with actions or words we might later regret.

3. You with the World
We live in this world. Of course we do! But it seems easy to forget with the demands of our daily lives. Our place here on planet earth is as citizens of a global community, both independently and interdependently on the earth. We share the planet with all beings as we co-exist, all dependent upon the sun for its life-giving radiance, warmth, and stabilizing gravitational force and upon the earth for its many resources.

As in the previous two relationships, we feel the residual effects of the yoga practice here. Over time, we develop and strengthen our felt sense (feelings internally perceived via sensations) and our emotional intelligence, or EQ. EQ is defined as the "capability of individuals to recognize their own emotions and those of others, discern between different feelings and label them appropriately, use emotional information to guide thinking and behavior, and manage and/or adjust emotions to adapt to environments or achieve one's goal(s)." [Wikipedia]

This seems strange, right? That yoga, meditation, and mindfulness can actually increase our empathy and compassion? But it's real and measured! Sara Lazar's scientific research in this area led to a highly popular video on YouTube (Lazar, 2015).

Studies have shown that EQ is more important than our IQ (Intelligence Quotient) for being successful in our jobs and family. As we improve our EQ, that in turn raises our sensitivity and increases our connection to the world at large via empathy and compassion.

The way we see it, even if you do not awake each day and recite the yamas and niyamas, yoga will touch you and sensitize you…in a good way!

4. You with your Spirit

It's interesting how uncomfortable people can be as soon as the words "spirit" or "spirituality" are mentioned. It's important to note that yoga predates all organized religions, but yoga itself is *not* a religion; there is no deity or god, per se. However, it can strengthen your beliefs in your religion. Interesting! How, though?

Since yoga is an empirical science and emphasizes personal experience through continuous practice and inquiry, it reveals ourselves to ourselves. By observing, assessing, and adjusting our relationships as noted above, we begin to touch our spiritual connection. Consider, for example, the idea of removal of the senses. This is a process of stepping back from sensory input, focusing attention inward, and listening internally. In doing so over a period of time, we connect to an inner knowing, and this inner knowing strengthens whatever it is you believe to be true.

Perhaps for an atheist it's simply a confirmation of disbelief, but it might also lead to a deeper insight of self and true inner essence. For an agnostic, it may reveal a specific higher source. For the polytheist or monotheist, yoga will enhance and complement your relationship to your spiritual belief system.

The Yoga Sutras provide a strong hint as to the importance of the spiritual side, or a connection to that which is larger than us. In both the first and second chapters, we find reference to Ishvara Pranidhana, devotion to divine presence. Depending upon which translation you read, this will reference devotion to God, the Lord, the Universe, or Supreme Consciousness.

The Yoga Sutras, and yoga itself, are not about religion or changing your religion. In our experience, however, yoga has strengthened our spirit. It has opened our awareness of the miracles that surround us. It has opened us to the miracle of the present moment and how all possibilities exist in the present moment. We are here in this embodied life to learn, love, and shine our light—to leave this planet better than it was when we arrived. To practice yoga is to be on a journey of realization.

• • •

Yoga is a means by which we examine all of our relationships in a very methodical way. Our body and breath are our most tangible assets for this process because both live in the present moment. Yoga reveals the nature of these relationships and provides a means to reconnect and remember who we are. This is what true yoga is. It's a technology like no other. You do not tap into these relationships through workouts at the gym or other fitness regimes.

EVERYTHING IS ENERGY

That pretty much says it all! It's a paraphrase of Albert Einstein's now famous quote:

> *Everything is energy and that's all there is to it.*
> *Match the frequency of the reality you want and you*
> *cannot help but get that reality. It can be no other way.*
> *This is not philosophy. This is physics.*

His words contain so much wisdom. There is potential energy, kinetic energy, chemical energy, electrical energy, electro-magnetic energy, thermal and solar energy—energies of all types. *We* are energy. Even our thoughts, feelings, and emotions are energy. (For a quick clarification, *emotions* are physical and instinctual, such as smiling or fear; *feelings* are mental associations or reactions to those emotions.)

To say everything is energy is also to say that the energy is everywhere. A similar ancient reference from the Upanishads is the reference of "I am that" or "Thou art that;" alternatively, in the Sanskrit, *So Hum* or *Tat Tvam Asi*. Consider that if all is energy and energy is everywhere, then *I* am energy, it's everywhere, and therefore I am that. *We* are that.

Here lies a great lesson that most of us miss. As we see the world, we should see ourselves. There is a little bit of each of us in everyone else, as we are all one. When we point our finger at someone, we need to remember there are three (quite literally the middle, ring, and pinky fingers of our pointing hand!) pointing back at us.

Continuing with this line of thinking, there is another interesting connection to the Upanishads: the concept of wholeness and completeness. So many of us feel lacking or insufficient in terms of our total being. Perhaps social media is a contributor as it's a "look at me" or "look at what I have or done" channel. People tend to bias their posts toward the good and not post about the bad day they are having. Looking at the stream of posts from most people could give the impression that their lives are just full of rainbows and unicorns, but of course this would not be the whole true story. This constant exposure to what appears to be everyone else in the world having it all can create a misperception for many of us that we are falling short, and are not whole, full, or complete.

The Sanskrit word *purnam* refers to wholeness, fullness, and completeness as well as to perfection. The Purnam chant of the Brihadaranyaka Upanishad in Sanskrit goes as follows:

> Om purnamadah, purnamidam
> Purnat purnamudachyate
> Purnasya purnamadaya
> Purnamevavasisyate
> Om Shanti, Shanti, Shanti

Loosely translated, it means, "This is whole, that is whole; from wholeness comes wholeness; that which is left is whole and that which is taken is whole." You can likewise substitute completeness or perfection for wholeness in this chant and it would mean the same.

The Purnam chant is very useful as a healing chant as its message is powerful. It means that all is whole, complete, or perfect. Making it personal, we are *each* whole, full, complete, and perfect as we are. *Everything* is perfect, both the entirety *and* the parts of the entirety. Perhaps a good analogy for the Purnam chant is to consider how a glass of sea water is just like the ocean, with the same qualities, elements, and aspects as the whole.

We often weave into our teaching this idea that we are perfect as we are. Each one of us is a miraculous creation and is full, complete, and whole. It was this ancient teaching that brought this realization out for us, and is not only a pillar of our teaching but also a message that we are spreading through our daily lives and travels.

Now, back to Einstein's quote. There is more, and this is awesome! He says, *Match the frequency of the reality you want and you cannot help but get it*. Whoa, sound familiar? That's like the Law of Attraction and the Law of Cause and Effect. In the case of the Law of Attraction, we receive that which we put out. If we are negative or intense, then negativity or intensity will be reflected back. The Law of Cause and Effect states that for every action or non-action, there is an effect or a reaction.

There are a lot of so-called "new age" ideas about this (e.g. The Secret, etc.) that have become popular…but, as Einstein said, this is simply physics! These concepts are thousands of years old and have never been hidden or secret.

We have the power to create our reality! It's up to us. Think about it. With each breath, each moment, each day that we wake, and each event in our lives, we have a chance to choose to be positive or negative. What we choose defines our emotions, feelings, and thoughts, which in turn project (cause) an energetic signature. This energetic signature then interacts with the world around us and results in an action or reaction (effect).

These laws, along with Einstein's quote, remind us of the importance of our relationships and of how we are relating to and defining our interactions with life as it passes by, moment by moment. In addition, Einstein's quote—and more importantly, all of his great work—brings validation to some of these ancient and thought-to-be esoteric concepts. In today's current culture, we relate to science better than ancient wisdom. Our contemporary view is through the eyes of the "show me" state. We need proof, validation, and evidence in order to believe. So it took the words of a genius such as Albert Einstein to awaken the world to the reality that has always been. Everything is energy!

A YOGIC PERSPECTIVE OF ENERGY AND THE CONCEPTUAL MODEL OF THE BODY

The views of yoga, Traditional Chinese Medicine, and Chinese and Japanese martial arts all have a similar view of energy. Energy is the life force, named *prana* in Sanskrit, *chi* in the Chinese traditions and *ki* in Japanese martial arts. How it is harnessed, experienced, and expressed varies by each tradition and modality.

In yoga, prana is related to breath, but it is more than simply the air we breathe. It's the universal life force. Conceptually, prana can be confusing to get your arms around. We obtain prana from the sun, the earth, and the air. Breathing is a physical indication of the vital energy working within us. In other words, prana is the underlying energy, the breath behind the breath. It's ethereal and essential. Prana acts as the fundamental life-giving force lying behind and through all living beings, just as gravity lies behind our ability to remain in perfect balance with the surface of the earth. We cannot measure or see prana, but we *can* measure the effects of prana. Brain waves and heart rate can be measured by scientific instrumentation (e.g., EEG, EKG, MRI, etc.), and these physiological effects are like living shadows of prana at work within us. Without prana, living beings and organisms die.

In yogic philosophy, the energies of our bodies—or, more accurately, our beings—flow through an elaborate system of channels called nadis. Prana flows through these channels as well. Depending upon which early text you reference, there are estimated to be between 72,000 and 350,000 nadis. The idea of nadis is a parallel belief and philosophy to the Chinese perspective of chi and meridians. More recent research and investigations associate the fascia and connective tissues as perhaps the primary conduits for the flow of energy throughout our body (Grilley, 2012).

For the purpose of self-realization, it was determined that only three main nadis mattered and are the focus. The first is the Sushumna Nadi, which runs along the spine and is the central channel. Running helically around this central channel are the Ida and Pingala channels, which carry the energetic qualities of our lunar and solar aspects, respectively. Balancing the energies of the Ida and Pingala Nadis is a key point of a yoga practice and leads to the clean and clear flow of energies to release stagnation throughout the entire system.

KOSHAS –WE ARE LAYERED BEINGS

In addition to these channels, we are composed of energetic layers, known in Sanskrit as koshas, or sheaths. The Taittiriya Upanishad (c. 700 BCE, Easwaran, 2007) first presents the concept that we are layered beings. A Russian doll is a nice visual analogy. Imagine multiple layers of energy encapsulating each other in the form of our human structure. However, each layer is interdependent on and interrelated to the others.

Through practicing yoga, we have become acutely aware of energy in these very terms—that is, through the deep awareness that yoga has brought us, we can now sense and feel the layers of our being.

There are five koshas:

1. **Annamaya Kosha:** Food layer. Here is the layer we most relate to, our outermost layer. This is our physical body, which—when you think about it—is the accumulation of all the foods you eat, all the lotions and oils you put on your skin, all the pollution you breathe, and all the medications, pills, or drugs you might intake. Here is a sobering thought, however: This sheath has a shelf life and is in constant decay starting from the moment we are born. The issue with this sheath is how we manage it and how its state of being interacts with the other sheaths.

   Annamaya kosha, the exterior layer, also emits energy outward, beyond the skin. This emitted energy is known as the aural field. Some researchers indicate this radiance extends as much as six feet or more beyond our skin as an electromagnetic field. Consider that the next time you are in an elevator or crowded room: Like it or not, you are sharing your energy and receiving energy from others without a word being spoken!

2. **Pranamaya Kosha:** Energy sheath. This is the first inner, unseen layer. Here is where the prana flows, making its way through our entire being.

3. **Manomaya Kosha:** Home of our mental faculties. This is the second inner layer, the layer of thoughts and memories, a storehouse of sorts with a positive, neutral, or negative polarity. As such, this layer may be supportive of our happiness and wellbeing—or not. Here is where our habits and patterns reside, called *samskaras* in Sanskrit. This sheath is arguably the most challenging to harmonize for overall wellness and ultimate enlightenment.

4. **Vijnanamaya Kosha:** Center of the intellect, personality, and val-

ues, the third deepest layer. Here is where wisdom resides. This layer is about discernment and is home to our personality and core values.

5. **Anandamaya Kosha:** Seat of emotion, happiness, and bliss. This deepest, final internal layer is certainly not the least; in fact, it's the one most of us want to experience and express! But here's the deal: How the other four layers are doing and how they interact and influence each other in turn affects this kosha in a positive or negative way.

Consider the koshas as layers of the "onion of our being," with each radiating and penetrating the neighboring layer. Enlightenment and purification through yoga works on these layers, like peeling the onion layers away so as to enhance our ability to tap into Anandamaya Kosha.

PRANA VAYUS: A WEATHER BAROMETER FOR HEALTH AND WELLNESS

Let's come back to the idea of prana. Understanding the nature and qualities of energy and the life force was the foundation upon which the science and technologies of yoga were developed and evolved. Think of prana as flowing through your body and see if you can visualize it moving like rivers and streams. In nature, rivers, streams, and large bodies of water may flow gently in a soft breeze, or flow with violent turbulent waves in stormy weather. Our states of health, our wellbeing, and our lifestyles determine the weather pattern in which our prana flows and is directly related to the state of our physiology and psychology. "Turbulence," in this case, refers to the state of our body and/or mind.

Using the weather analogy provides a simple and visual way to see how the body-mind system interacts. Consider an example: It's easy to imagine that if you had a bad day at work, the related stress would perhaps manifest as tension in the hips and neck. It might raise your cortisol levels and blood pressure. These negative physiological reactions to the stress of the day would create stormy weather and turbulent winds (i.e., negative energy) which would have a negative effect on the flow of prana. This analogy provides a barometer of health and wellness. We want our inner weather to be calm with gentle breezes and clear blue skies just as we do outside.

Vayus is the Sanskrit for *winds*. Wind is energy and it brings movement. In the yogic conceptual model, there are five types of prana vayu. Each vayu carries or moves prana in a dedicated way for a specific function.

1. **Prana Vayu** is the inward- and upward-lifting life force and determines movement
2. **Apana Vayu** refers to the downward life force governing elimination
3. **Samana Vayu** controls assimilation and discernment
4. **Udana Vayu** controls our expression
5. **Vyana Vayu** is about circulation and expansion

Collectively, these five vayus distribute prana throughout our being. We use the word "being" and not "body" because prana flows throughout all the koshas, not just within the physical body.

The interrelatedness of the body and breath (prana) is not a new concept. Another view of this comes from The Hatha Yoga Pradipika (Muktibodhananda, 1993), another classic yoga text which, paraphrased, says, "As is the breath, so is the mind, and as is the mind, so is the breath."

WHAT IN THE WORLD IS A CHAKRA?

Among the many subjects of yoga, the chakras are most fascinating for us. Derived from the concept of energy flowing through rivers and streams within our being, it is logical that at juncture points, multiple channels will converge to create a vortex of concentrated energy. These vortex centers, called chakras, vary in size and are distributed throughout the body. Some are major, some minor. These vortices carry both physiological and psychological qualities. So you can imagine that bad energetic weather or turbulent winds will also affect the chakra centers.

It's worth taking a pause here to note that this is a conceptual model. While we can feel, sense, and even scientifically measure the effects and manifestations of the human energy system, it's unseen. It's energetic! You cannot dissect a human and find the chakra centers. However, the concept of energy centers within the body cuts across the traditions of Yoga, Buddhism, and Jainism. Furthermore, the concept is not limited to India; similar philosophies existed in ancient Egypt and with the Mayans as well as with the indigenous peoples of North and South America (Dale, 2009).

It's also interesting that the locations of these centers very nearly coincide with key organs of the endocrine system and the nerve plexuses. In addition, the nature and qualities of the charkas directly relate to the physical and chemical aspects of the organs. Now, certainly the ancient sages did not have the scientific methods and measurement technologies of today, but through empirical and experiential means they developed a conceptual model which is proving to be a reasonable qualitative model with scientific validity.

The common and most widely accepted theory presents seven chakra centers that rest in the Pranamaya Kosha and are located along the spine, anchored in the central Sushumna Nadi channel. Each chakra is said to be a vortex with a uniform spin when healthy, and an otherwise non-uniform, unsteady spin when unhealthy.

The chakras and the related network of nadi energy channels radiate energy. We like to think of the chakras as knitting across the Koshas that interconnect the physical, psychological, and spiritual aspects of our total being.

HATHA—THE DANCE OF OUR SOLAR AND LUNAR ENERGIES

Hatha is the Sanskrit word containing both Sun (Ha) and Moon (Tha). Hatha Yoga emphasizes the balancing of the solar and lunar energies. This dual orientation of extremes is connected to our brains. The left hemisphere of the brain controls the right side of our body, which is the solar aspect containing Pingala nadi. The right hemisphere controls the left side of our body, which contains Ida nadi. These lunar and solar, right and left, hemispheres of the brain should be in balance for overall health, happiness, and wellness.

The challenge with our western culture and lifestyle is that most of us are in overdrive and are living out of balance, typically with too much solar, dynamic, masculine energy. We are operating in a state of fight or flight, with high cortisol levels and adrenaline, amped up and ready to jump at a moment's notice. Over long periods of time, running on overdrive manifests as illness and eventually disease.

> *Dennis*: For me, I consider Hatha as an energetic dance of the lunar and solar aspects of my being. Running too hot (solar) or too cold (lunar) is not good in the long haul. Either extreme is not sustainable. The lesson of balancing energies within us is foundational to the practice of yoga.

WE ARE SPIRITUAL BEINGS HAVING A TEMPORARY HUMAN EXPERIENCE

Considering our energetic anatomy—composed of the koshas, prana vayus, chakras, nadis, and the aural field extending beyond the surface of our skin—we are truly amazing beings. Each of these elements has its own energetic nature, but each interacts and influences the others.

Since we are energetic beings, it could be said that we are spiritual beings having a temporary human experience. As energy cannot be created nor destroyed, then that inner essence, the Anandamaya kosha, is everlasting. Our physical, embodied lives are limited, but our essence is limitless. The ancient practices of yoga are the integrated technologies that tune us not just for this lifetime, but for our transformation beyond this life!

This was another key teaching of yoga for us. We find peace and comfort knowing that it's all about energy and we are empowered with the practices of yoga to direct, manage, and improve our lifestyles in a way that's beneficial to those around us and the earth that supports us.

THE NATURE OF THE MIND

"Chitta vritti nirodha," YS 1.2
— Yoga is mastering the modifications of the mind

As the second of 195 aphorisms (196 by some interpretations) in the Yoga Sutras (Bryant, 2009), this Sutra says it plainly: Yoga is mastery over the fluctuations, or modifications—the "chitta"—of the mind. When we first read the Yoga Sutras, we could not help but notice that most of it is about the mind. Other historical texts such as the Upanishads, the Bhagavad Gita, and the Hatha Yoga Pradipika are also mostly concerned with the mind. How we relate to and manage our mind determines our inter-relationship in the world. It starts with us, our own mind, then yoga works on our lifestyles off the mat. How we are in the world is all up to us!

What is the nature of the mind? What is the mind-body connection and how does it work? These questions have plagued humanity for thousands of years. The mind is a mystery and is the subject of ongoing research that continues today. However, there has been great progress over the past century that provide glimpses into revealing just how powerful the mind is.

MIND: THE SPACIOUS LIMITLESS UNIVERSE OF OUR BRAINS

So how does the mind work? Our life experience is a function of our perceptions via our senses, but is also tied to our upbringings, traditions, past-life memories, inherited karmas, tribal knowledge, and culture. For example, Dennis grew up in a small rural setting in Massachusetts with a New England Protestant religious view, whereas Kathy grew up in Daytona Beach, Florida, with a Baptist view. We inherited different genetics and had very different upbringings which created impressions which still influence how we interpreted and interacted with the world. And by "culture," we don't just mean that of your neighborhood or town, but also of your state and nation.

Let's step back and begin with the external. The world around us just *is*. It is there with or without us. We perceive the world to be a certain way because of our relationship WITH it... not because of the world itself. It's our relationship or connection with the external that we impart and project upon the world. We interpret the world through our life experiences and perceptions.

Therefore, our internal world, i.e., our experience or so-called "reality," is defined by our consciousness, which is an integration of our ideas, thoughts, feelings, etc. Much of our consciousness is very subjective and personal. Whereas the external world is objective, it simply *is*.

Awareness has three components: physical, mental, and emotional. The physical aspect includes our sense perceptions. Through sight, sound, touch, smell, and taste we collect inputs from the external world. These inputs are physical and objective inputs that are collected and processed within the brain, but then the mind gets involved and interprets this data. For example, you might taste something and decide you like it and want more of it. But your liking of a certain flavor is largely affected by your upbringing, tribe, tradition, and culture. Having traveled overseas a lot, we've experienced diets in other cultures that include food we would not eat here in the United States. It's not that our foods or their diets are wrong; they're just different. Likewise with smells, sights, and all other sensory input.

The mental component of awareness includes our thoughts, knowledge, and experience. These come from our past but they project onto the present, leading to opinions of whatever is happening right now. Everything we have lived and experienced in the past is stored and leaves impressions within our minds, brains, and even the tissues of our bodies (psychosomatically), leading us to make decisions in the present. We have an amazing ability to quickly compare new experiences, seemingly instantaneously, with our past experiences, and then assess them accordingly. A simple example might be choosing to avoid a certain way home from the office based upon past experiences.

Past thoughts and experiences can be good as they might guide us toward a least-effort experience. But those thoughts and experiences might be based upon false assumptions and limited information. In this case, perhaps the route home previously had road construction that is now clear and is in fact the fastest route.

The third component of awareness is emotional. This touches upon our inner being and moves toward our intuitive or subjective feeling. There is an exciting direction of research which cuts across the disciplines of neural biology, psychology, and neural science and looks at how "following our gut," or intuition, is actually real, valid, and tied to the brain. Our emotional awareness is at least equally important as our physical and mental awareness. It's through emotional sensitivity that we can interpret and assess an outside-world experience with our intuition.

Kathy: Back in September 1994, when we were in the corporate world, my job required me to travel quite a bit. We were living in Richmond, Virginia, at the time and I was taking a business trip to Chicago for the day to meet with a customer. I flew USAir from Richmond to Chicago via Pittsburg and got on the rental car bus to go pick up a car. While on the bus, I got a strong feeling—not really the big, booming voice of God, but a definite, powerful unspoken message said, "Do not rent a car."

At first, I tried not to listen because my logical brain was saying, "You have to rent a car to drive to see this customer," but the voice got so loud that I had to change my plans. When the rental car bus got to the Hertz lot, I told the driver that I needed to go back to the terminal to catch a cab. Once there, I jumped in a cab to go to my appointment about an hour away. I had barely enough cash to pay the driver—and back then, cabs did not take credit cards and there was no Uber or Lyft. This was 1994! Very worried about how in the world I was going to get back to the airport, I begged the driver to come back for me in an hour. My logical brain again said, "There is no way this cab is going to hang around this part of Chicago for an hour for you. You will never see him again." But sure enough, as I was wrapping up my meeting, I looked out the window and I saw that same cabbie pulling up to get me. I was so stunned and thrilled! He took me to an ATM so I could get more cash, we had a smooth ride back to the airport, and I was ahead of schedule. I was able to take an earlier flight home through Pittsburgh because I didn't spend extra time renting the car.

That evening, I got a call from a co-worker asking how my trip to Chicago went. He seemed overly concerned and I told him "Great! I even got home earlier than expected." I asked him why he sounded worried and he explained that USAir flight 427 from Chicago to Pittsburgh had crashed that day and all 132 people on board were killed.

I had a ticket in my hand for that flight.

I believe that if I had ignored my intuition or the strong message/gut feeling that told me not to rent a car, I would have been one of those 132 people. So from that day forward, I have always listened to my intuition and paid attention to those gut feelings as they have saved my life.

Some of us are more naturally intuitive than others, although our intuitive connections can be developed and cultivated.

• • •

These three aspects of awareness—physical, mental, and emotional—together filter or add color to the world around us. Data from the external world enters via our awareness, which is a mind-body process. Our awareness—via perception, sensations, thoughts, feelings, and emotions—defines our own personal experience in the world, our own "maya" (Sanskrit for illusion). We have all heard of seeing the world through rose-colored glasses. We all experience our own maya as seen through our own version of colored glasses.

Now here is the interesting part. Inside our own minds, we capture the input data and decide: Do we like it or not? Everything we experience falls into one of these categories. You see, we live in a world of opposites or duality. Ancient sages and teachers have written and taught about this for millennia. The things we like we want more of, and the things we do not like, we want less of. We become attached to our likes, which is known as *attachments*. We want to avoid what we do not like, and this is known as *aversions*.

Consider these as two buckets in which most of us place each and every experience. Like/don't like. Attachment/aversion. But this is more than just buckets or place holders. We react and respond to our experiences through the lens of our likes and dislikes. On top of that, our ego gets involved as well, driven by the need for personal importance and self-esteem. And since we, as humans, are great storytellers, we justify our actions based upon what feeds our egos.

Now, do not confuse our point here. Our opinion is not that the ego is necessarily bad. Self-esteem, importance, and promotion are positive elements for our life in the world. They provide drive and guidance. Ego is basic to our survival. However, when these elements become obsessive and operate at the expense of others (remember, yoga is about relationships), that's when the ego gets out of control. It's this negative part of the ego, the part which is a very good storyteller, a good salesman of sorts, that jumps in to justify our position or our actions.

> *Dennis*: During one of my last business trips to Washington, DC before Kathy and I resigned, an associate at a dinner meeting accused me of being a "deep thinker." It was said with a negative undertone. Still, to this day, I recall this conversation and I often wonder, what did he mean? Like, is it better in his opinion to be a shallow thinker? Or was my deep thinking over his head, or did

he think it wasn't fit for the corporate culture? This was one of several conversations that confirmed my need to make a change. Through the years, Kathy often jokingly calls me a deep thinker when I get all nerdy on her.

Ego, attachment, and aversion also create discontent as well as a fear of letting go—which is arguably one of the most important (if not *the* most important) issues we all face whether we recognize it or not. Fear of letting go manifests in all aspects of our lives. Let's take career change. How many people do you know who are not satisfied with or happy in their jobs? Of those, how many have actually taken steps to do something about it? Probably not that many. Our comfort zones are connected to fear of letting go, as we are concerned with the unknown. Paradoxically, discontent can arise from staying in our comfort zone, as in the case of the career change.

Also, there is the fear of death. Okay, we said it. Yes, generally speaking, we all have a fear of death. For some, it's a very serious affliction that causes the painful concern on a daily basis. From the day we were born, we all have been dying. The issue can dramatically influence how we relate to this reality. Fear of death is the ultimate fear of letting go.

We do not know how long we will be here and by what means will we depart; it's a great mystery of life. Since there is no way of getting out of here alive, why don't we accept it and focus on the present moment, thankful for each moment we have? Of course, that's been a main issue of humanity since we all learned how to walk on our two feet!

These afflictions—ego story telling of *I, me, mine*; attachments; aversions; fear of letting go; fear of death—together create a mind state which results in patterns of reaction and actions. Repeated patterns become habits. Habits can become addictions.

The ancient yogis have a beautiful word for this: *samskaras*. Samskaras refer to the mental impressions, grooves, or scars that we create in our brain as we repeat the same behavior over and over. The word samskara comes from the Sanskrit "sam" (complete or joined together) and "kara" (action, cause, or doing). Repeating samskaras, positive or negative, reinforces them, creating a groove that is difficult to resist.

People get caught in the pull of destructive samskaras for many reasons. Humans seek comfort in the familiar even if it is not serving them well anymore. Many times, we are not aware of the negative habitual pattern until we start to look inward and intentionally try to know ourselves better. The fourth Niyama (Self-study or Svadhyaya) is all about this.

By working with different techniques, we can learn how to recognize when thoughts or actions are more harmful than beneficial and how to stop them from occurring. The brain's cognitive processes will be re-wired and retrained to develop new samskaras that are productive, rational, and positive.

In the Western medicine context, samskaras are the neural pathways that are wired into our grey matter and become repeated responses or reactions to situations or triggers encountered. Every moment of every day, we are firing off neural pathways as we react and respond to our life experiences.

SO MANY THOUGHTS, BUT MOST ARE WORTHLESS

Separate from external inputs that come from the physical world, the brain is a thought generator. Thoughts are internally generated and may be connected to past memories, current moment stimuli from the senses, or plans for the future.

We have about 50,000 thoughts per day (Huffington Post, the Blog, 5/23/2013), and some studies say 70,000. On the low side, that's over 2,000 thoughts per hour, more than thirty per minute, or about one thought every two seconds. YIKES! That's a lot of thinking, thinking, thinking! Here is the kicker: Most of these thoughts are useless or are thoughts we have repeated over and over again!

Thoughts of the past are just a waste of time, as the past is over, but these thoughts still manifest in most of us as worry, regret, and depression. Contrasting this, being concerned or anxious about the future is also a time-waster as the future isn't here yet and we cannot control the outcome. To add to that, negative thoughts are like velcro and stick with us, but positive thoughts are like teflon and slide away.

The mind ingests and digests data, yet it's fundamentally fearful, is constantly generating useless thoughts, and is a great storyteller. So what's a person to do?

The answer lies with revisiting our awareness from a slightly different angle. Remember, yoga is about relationships. The way to work with the mind is to find awareness that we are in a relationship with the exterior world, but simultaneously also with our own internal world via physical, mental, and emotional aspects.

Through awareness we can see and sense. We can observe and notice. When we are observing with awareness, we can insert a pause in our lives where we need it, thereby shifting our reactivity into a more deliberate response. It's these simple, small steps, taken in this way, that begin creating change in our relationships, our awareness, and our consciousness.

The old saying that old dogs cannot learn new tricks is wrong. The latest research (Lazar, 2015) has shown that, in fact, old dogs *can* learn new tricks. Neuroplasticity is the scientific term for the brain's ability to rewire itself—that is to say, create new neural pathways which define new responses and reshape old habits. The Lazar study showed that with meditation and yoga, the typical shrinking of gray matter in the pre-frontal cortex that happens as we age—and the pre-frontal cortex is the part of our brain responsible for working memory and executive decision making—is slowed down or prevented. Her study proves that meditation can actually *change the size* of key regions of our brain, improving our memory and making us more empathetic, compassionate, and resilient under stress.

In addition, we can shift our relationship to our thoughts through contemplative and mindfulness practices. The brain is going to produce thoughts all the time, so it's not about stopping the thoughts. Rather, these practices teach us to notice our thoughts but not engage them, and to observe the present moment without judgement. It's so interesting that our minds paint a unique image of our experiences; our minds are where our issues or afflictions originate and reside; and our minds is where our own answers lie.

WHEREVER YOU GO, THERE YOU ARE

As the quote says, *Wherever you go, there you are.* You cannot get away from yourself. Certainly the brain is connected to the rest of the physical body. The brain keeps us alive via the autonomic nervous system. The heart pumps, lungs breathe, oxygen is exchanged, our eyes see, we touch and feel, we taste, ingest, and digest food, the environment, and our life experiences. And we do not even have to think about these functions, as they miraculously just happen.

Remember, our brain is an organ that is like command central, functioning automatically without our input; it's our *minds* that create our unique living experiences. The mind is the key aspect of our being—our consciousness, through which we filter, store, and experience our world.

During a creative writing session that we hosted at our home, the teacher led us through an exercise in which each of us was asked to write what we saw in the room. This was to be an "as-is" writing assignment: Simply write what you see with no judgement or interpretation. There were eight of us taking the class in the room. After about fifteen minutes of writing, we shared what we wrote. You guessed it: There were eight different views of what was in the room. Each person, although in the very same environment, had their own individual experiences.

This is not unique to this creative writing class or the attendees at the time. This is common to the human experience. It's not the brain that causes this; it's the mind. Everything we take in through our senses, our sensory inputs, are filtered by the mind based upon our own interpretation. From the yogic point of view, this is *maya*, or illusion.

PRACTICES

THE NATURE OF PRACTICE

"Practice and all is coming."
— *Sri K. Pattabhi Jois*

K. Pattabhi Jois developed and popularized Ashtanga yoga, which was the style of the very first class we took. Perhaps this is his most famous quote. His other famous quote is, "Yoga is ninety-nine percent practice and one percent knowledge." Together these provide the foundation of yoga: You can study and theorize, but at the end of the day it's all about practice. The more you practice, the more all will come.

As we considered this over the years, we have come to see yoga as an empirical science. The traditions and foundations of yoga through the ages were founded upon intuition and experience. In recent times, say the past century, our "prove it to me first/validation only" culture has confirmed through scientific methods that these ancient practices are indeed valid. We are amazed and awed by the continued research and studies that drill into the systematic methods of yoga, meditation, and mindfulness.

If you were to gaze through the front window of a yoga studio while class is in session, it would be easy to make certain assumptions. Without context, a yoga practice looks like a series of postures that are linked together in some way. To some, it might look easy and simple, as most of the postures themselves are not really complex. Even the so-called advanced postures, which might take on more of a Cirque du Soleil impression and seem out of reach of the mere mortal, would look simply gymnastics-like.

However, this cursory view would miss the point. As with the iceberg analogy, there is more below the surface of a yoga practice. In this section on practice, we are addressing the deeper, hidden aspects of yoga. We are not writing about new poses, sequences, or some newly contrived style of yoga but rather are presenting our view of how to integrate yoga into your daily life, on and off the mat, in order for you to be happier and healthier, and perhaps find your true essence.

PRACTICE MAKES PERFECT: GOOD OR BAD

You know the old saying, "Practice makes perfect"? You've probably heard it a gazillion times and know that it means regularly doing an activity or skill to become proficient. Many times it relates to playing a musical instrument or doing a physical activity. Back when we were kids, the saying was used for things like penmanship, spelling, or learning the multiplication tables. As yogis, we can get caught up in a practice makes perfect mentality to nail that difficult arm balance or achieve the gravity-defying jump back.

Let's just look at the word *practicing*, which Wikipedia defines as "rehearsing a behavior over and over, or engaging in an activity again and again, for the purpose of improving or mastering it." If we choose to look at this word in a different way and apply it to the *mind* instead of the body, we can sometimes get a rude awakening.

As mindfulness teacher and researcher Dr. Shana Shapiro would ask, "*What* are you practicing?" We had the privilege of attending a mindfulness retreat she led at Esalen in December 2015. Among the many subjects covered, her points regarding practice really resonated with us.

For example, what are you practicing mentally all day? Is it judgement, anxiousness, worry, depression, pessimism, comparison, perfectionism, selfishness, cynicism, and neuroticism? If so, those traits are getting stronger and you are mastering them. Is that what you want? So shouldn't we all practice more compassion, kindness, integrity, loyalty, respectfulness, humility, forgiveness, generosity, optimism, and lovingness, so these get stronger?

All of life is a practice. We are all practicing in each moment of our existence. Take time throughout the day to check in with your thoughts, notice what is happening, and decide if that is what you want to perfect.

Consider, for example, the driver who cuts you off as you try to merge into traffic. The immediate unenlightened reaction is one of frustration and anger, most likely involving several vulgarities mixed with inappropriate sign language. In this example, at the moment of the occurrence, practice is ongoing and you are getting better at frustration and anger, deepening those samskaras grooves. This reaction is a practice in mindless interruption. But was this reaction necessary? Was it effective?

PERSONAL PRACTICE:
WHERE THE RUBBER MEETS THE ROAD

Everyone who practices yoga should have a personal practice.

A personal practice, or home practice, is one you do alone at home or while traveling. It does not need to be elaborate or even long, like a studio class. It can be very simple, just getting on the floor, even without a mat (God forbid!). Remember that whether in a studio or at home, a yoga practice includes all aspects of yoga—which is to say, all elements of the eight limbs of the Yoga Sutras.

Practicing yoga asana in a group setting is easier, in a sense, as you are guided throughout the practice. However, have you ever felt like the playlist was wrong or you would rather not have music? Or the sequencing was too strong and dynamic or too light and gentle for you that day?

A home practice can take on many forms of mindful movement and does not have to be ninety minutes of power vinyasa flow. In fact, it most likely will not be.

Making the practice your own is ultimately what it's all about. As we have said, yoga is very personal. Once you have been practicing in a studio for a while, try it out on yourself. Do not be concerned that you are not a teacher or that you might hurt yourself. Personal practice is about listening, feeling, and expressing from within with discernment. That is, acknowledge that each day we come to the mat as we are and give yourself permission to follow your intuition and be guided by sensations as they arise.

Personal practice integrates spontaneous movement with synchronized breath and intention. Coupled with mindful awareness, right attention, and right attitude, this will lead to a yoga practice that taps deeper below the surface.

Allow the body to flow and float upon the breath. *Feel (*via your body intelligence) and *express (*via your intuitive connection) the practice rather than force it. Get out of your left brain, the analytical side, and be free with your practice. With this integrated approach, physical asana takes on the advanced form of practice.

Let's address two concerns you might have.

1. **Injury**: Most yoga injuries happen in studios—not because of the teacher, but because of the practitioner's ego getting in the way. This goes right back to the Yoga Sutras. One of our afflictions is this tendency to let the ego take charge and push or force us into or out of a pose. Forcing is a form of violence; in this case, the violence is toward yourself as you force yourself into a pose at the risk of injury. The Sutras—specifically ahimsa or nonviolence—became a guidance system for our practice. Both the transitions between the poses and the poses themselves must be executed mindfully, without excessively pushing toward achievement and without force. Seek to optimize and shift energy such that there is both effort and ease.

2. **Alignment**: Some traditions, styles, and studios place a major emphasis on physical, anatomical alignment. We appreciate the concern, but we also feel we should give our nervous and respiration systems credit. They are intelligent. They cross-communicate neurologically, chemically, and even electromagnetically in the present moment, and they do not lie. The challenge we all deal with is to listen. Listening to the body is a skill that is improved with practice.

With these two points in mind, let's discuss and consider the nature and key elements of a personal practice.

- Center, get grounded, and tune in. It is very important to tune in and begin the practice from the right place. This sets the tone of the practice. Centering can happen in a seated position, lying on your back or belly, in sage pose (sitting on your heels), or even standing. This process might last just a few minutes, but it is absolutely key.

- While centering, shift your mind from *thinking and doing* to *being and sensing*. With this step, we start to tap into taking the practice from a surface level experience to something deeper. Become the observer or witness who is actively listening to all the senses, feelings, and emotions that arise during the practice.

- Transition your breath to Ujjayi breath. This is the classical breath used in most yoga practices. Breathe this way by gently restricting the glottis or back of the throat to restrict both the inhalation and the exhalation, thereby lengthening the breath and slowing down your respiration. In doing so, the lengthened exhale triggers the parasympathetic nervous system, causing the relaxation response.

This retraction of the glottis is physiologically the same thing we do when we whisper, so if it helps, you can imagine whispering the word "ahhhh" on both the inhale and exhale. If you're new to this, do it with the mouth open until you have a feel for it, and then close the mouth and breathe through the nose only.

Ujjayi breath creates a gentle and soft audible breath that becomes the monitor of the practice. This gentle hissing sound is for you; it's not a form of performance. We have heard students breathing so loudly that they sound like bull alligators in heat! This is not necessary and could be viewed as another form of the ego getting in the way.

Watch the tempo or rhythm of your breath as well as the texture (smooth or rough). This will speak the truth of your experience. In other words, your breath should remain smooth and balanced throughout the entire practice. If it is rapid, irregular, or rough, that is often an indicator that you are pushing too hard and not being truthful with yourself.

- Breath is absolutely critical to yoga practice as it bridges the physical to the non-physical. As noted in the ancient texts, "So is the breath, so is the mind," and vice versa.

- In addition, the right attitude is important. Practicing yoga with a negative attitude or a closed mind is pointless and defeats the purpose. The wrong attitude will keep the practice at the surface and not allow for the opening and expansion which are essential to fully benefit from the practice. A positive and open attitude will facilitate lightness and fullness, which will cause a blooming of the experience.

- Entering a pose, use micro-adjustments and wriggles to find the right balance of effort and ease within the shape. Feel your way in; do not force your way. To *force* is to bring false expectations about the future state of your pose. To *feel* is to be connected to the present moment and to listen to sensations as they arise, including sensations of the tissues of your body and the tempo of your breath.

- Align your body into a pose for optimum load bearing. Also consider the direction of forces within the body to hold the shape. This is the physical aspect of the pose. One way to visualize and feel this alignment is to think of it in terms of "stacking your bones." If you consider each pose as a structure, and imagine you are taking the shape to hold for a while, this will help you find your fullest expression and feel for what *stacking the bones* means. This concept will minimize the tendency to allow off-axis rotations or other mis-alignments that might cause pain or injury. Most students think stacking the bones only applies when the legs are straight, but it also comes into play in Chair pose, Warrior poses, and especially in balances.

- Visualize your lines of energy within the shape and seek optimum energetic flow. For example, if you are simply standing with your legs straight, one line of energy runs directly from the hips along each leg, into the mat or floor. Another runs from the hips up along the spine and into the crown of the head. Visualizing the straight lines that direct efficient pathways for flow of energy will help you find and fine-tune your alignment.

- Thinking in terms of lines of energy and stacking the bones brings awareness of how the body is positioned in space and its relationship to gravity. A pose built upon energy optimization in this way will also facilitate proper breathing, as the diaphragm will be oriented for maximum utilization.

> *Kathy*: Can you tell by this wording that Dennis is a structural engineer by degree? Sorry if he reverts back to his inner nerd!

What he is saying is that you can visualize lines of energy to support you in the pose like the framing of a house supports the building. By the optimization of energy, he means find balance between *pushing* or *muscling* (and over-doing a shape) versus just limply holding the shape. The pose should consist of the whole body taking the shape, in a balanced way so that you could stay there for a while. Some styles of yoga hold standing postures upwards of ten to fifteen minutes! Finding the right balance of effort allows the body to sustain the shape.

- If you are aware of the seven chakra centers, then consider stacking them energetically the same as you would consider stacking the bones anatomically. Acknowledging your energetic anatomy enhances your alignment and magnifies the benefits of your yoga practice.

- For transitions, be very mindful of the motion as you shift the loads and energies of your body. Transitions actually carry the highest probability of injury! They are just as important as the pose itself and are sometimes more difficult. Keep the same aspects of awareness engaged throughout the motion you take to get into the next pose as you do to the pose itself.

- Personal practice is an opportunity to create your own practice that suits you that day, matching your energy as it is. Erich Schiffmann, a well-known Western yogi who has been teaching for decades, is known for his "Freedom Style Yoga." We had the opportunity to take several classes and immersions with him and just love how he begins by instructing with postural cues and then, after a period of time, opens it up for the students to do their own thing on their own mat. It's very freeing, especially in a group setting. For personal practice, you can create your own freedom style by simply letting yourself go.

Let your body move freely with no judgement. Let it be a free expression of yourself in the moment.

PERSONAL PRACTICE FOR THE BUSY PROFESSIONAL OR CORPORATE TRAVELER

There are many aspects of yoga that we love. One is that, really, you do not need anything but yourself. Remember: Wherever you go, there you are! You are always there wherever you are, so you can practice wherever you are. You do not need a $100 yoga mat or $150 worth of yoga attire. All you need is a conscious decision to practice and a little space, just enough to match your own size and movements.

> *Dennis*: While still in the crazy travel of my corporate days, when I was away from home two to three weeks of any given month, I would follow practices on DVDs and CDs on my laptop in my hotel rooms. If I could, I would also hit local studios where I was traveling, but often the daily schedule would not allow it. So I would practice in the room. I became pretty innovative at the use of the bathroom door frame as prop—or maybe more accurate to say, a support structure for practicing handstands. My early experiments and trials of doing a full wheel back-bend involved the bed in the hotel room, as I would let my torso hang off the edge and dangle to develop the back opening and hand/arm alignment. The wall was used for support in arm balances and inversions.

Whether you are a busy professional, a homemaker, or just a mere mortal who likes to travel, yoga goes with you. Today, with all the online resources, you have the greatest teachers and a universe of yoga styles and types available to be your virtual guide. All you need to do is make the decision to practice.

On a practical note, try not to eat for two to four hours before a physical yoga practice. Why? Well...

> *Kathy:* Early on in our practice, we were clueless about the usual guideline to not eat a heavy meal two to four hours before practicing, so we went to a well-known Mexican restaurant and both got giant bean burritos. We wolfed them down so we could get to yoga class on time. Let me tell you, that was really a bad idea, not only for our own bodies but for our fellow students. I apologize now to the people who had their mats near me. I was the most uncomfortable physically that I have ever been. Lesson learned!

A TYPE A PERSONALITY
MEETS SURYA NAMASKAR

Psychologists came up with the categories of type A, B, C, or D personalities based on certain traits. Type A tends to be driven and competitive, therefore susceptible to stress which leads to coronary heart disease and other illnesses. Type B is the opposite, with a more laid-back, casual approach; Type B lives in the present moment. Type C is detail- and structure-oriented and tends not to be assertive; this lack of assertiveness becomes a huge source of stress in their lives. Type D is overall distressed—these are folks who are highly negative, pessimistic, and worried. Not surprisingly, Type D is very likely to suffer from stress-related diseases as well.

We both had qualities of A and B, but it was a mix. Dennis' Type A characteristics outweighed his Type B tendencies, whereas Kathy had more B than A. It's probably one reason why we made such a good team, as our characteristics worked well together. That is, until Dennis' ego took over and became so enamored with his title, income, and frequent flyer points.

The ABCD approach to personalities is just one of several available. Of course there are the corporate human resources versions, which are widely used to categorize employees. During our careers, we were assessed by several methods. Perhaps the most notable was while we were employees of a large, multi-national public company which will remain nameless. They had a corporate-wide evaluation for all professional staff using a personality test that included measurement of our reactions under stress. The results were then placed on name badges for each employee to wear, so co-workers could see your category and stress response tendencies for the purpose of team building on various projects. Wow, that was interesting… and like many large corporate initiatives, this one did not gain much traction and actually caused concerns of some employees who felt inferior and psychologically violated.

We share this story simply to note that we have been assessed many times. And yet, as our awareness expanded through our yoga practice, we started to notice more accurately where we fell in the matrix of personality types. This came from self-study, observation, and certainly from noticing how we are on the mat. But, more importantly, it came from observing how we were off the mat in the real world of daily life. Dennis often refers to himself as a "recovering Type A"!

This self-observation seems to just happen if you stick with the practice long enough. If you truly do as the teacher says and allow yourself to let go, don't compare, be content, synchronize your breath, and be mindfully connected to sensations as they arise, changes will happen. This is some of the magic of yoga that we had not expected.

There's a very famous mantra, the Asatoma mantra, from the Upanishads that states:

May we be led from darkness to light,
May we be led from falsehood to truth,
May we be lead from poison to nectar.

This mantra provides the direction and guidance to purify ourselves, and it really is a purification that we go through in yoga. As the ancient text says, we shine light upon darkness, we find truth, and we detoxify the poison out of our body-mind system. And one of the main sequences of yoga, the Surya Namaskar (or "sun salutation") was the piece that, for Dennis, made the greatest early impact.

> *Dennis:* Personally, it was Surya Namaskar that really worked on me. Surya Namaskar is the name of a sequence of poses linked with transitions and breath that is continuous and often repeated over and over.
>
> "Surya" means *solar* and "namaskar" translates to *salutation;* therefore this refers to a salutation to the sun. There are several variations and adaptations of this sequence that have evolved over the years. Relative to the historic timeline of yoga, Surya Namaskar is fairly young, arriving on the scene in the early 1900s and credited to Krishnamacharya (1888 - 1989). No single version is better than another; they are just different and typically linked to a particular tradition. However, in essence, the sequence is a repetitive moving meditation and very potent when done with mindful awareness. It is absolutely a beautiful practice. If you knew nothing else, this would be enough.
>
> Surya Namaskar became my 12-step program as I would mentally go into this meditative safe place. It became the core of my practice. It was perfect for me as I needed nothing else once I knew it and put it into my body. The combination of breath, controlled movement (not too fast, not too slow), and mindful awareness took

me deep into myself. I would mentally hold a connection to the sun as the life-giving force of all and to the lunar aspects of myself as my practice would evolve. The practice became sacred and primal. Followed by a long Savasana, which really should be at least ten minutes, this practice makes your soul sing.

Yoga is ideal for all who suffer from stress. To alleviate it and manage stress with yoga, the practice does not have to be complex, difficult, or advanced. All it needs to be is practiced with the right attitude, awareness, and mindful presence.

HURTING IT MORE
WON'T MAKE IT HURT LESS

During our early days of practicing yoga we had brought with us the only approach to fitness that we knew. Each of us had experiences in athletic activities and sports from our youth, which had the common thread of competitiveness.

> *Dennis*: Although I had practiced martial arts, my interest favored the more competitive aspects. I studied Karate, Tae Kwon Do, Wing Chun, and Shaolin Kung Fu over the course of about six years from high school through college. Each style incorporated their meditative practices and the integration of energy, ki (Japanese) or chi (Chinese). It was the competitive side of sparring and forms that really resonated with me as it fed my need for building confidence.
>
> I was drawn to martial arts as I was an overweight, introverted kid who needed to improve my self-esteem and lose a few pounds. So my approach was firm and assertive, which became ingrained within me. I do credit martial arts with providing both the confidence and toning that I really needed which, in turn, laid the

foundation to pursue college and shaped me for success in my career.

Virtually all of the fitness activities in our culture engage an attitude taken from Darwin's concept of survival of the fittest. Survival of the fittest, by definition, requires competition and has become a mantra for some. Now add this to our dynamic, high speed, commercialized world, a world of iPhones, iPads, texting, and tweeting. A world in which the default settings of our lives tend toward this competitive drive, toward pushing through whatever is in our way and working from an attitude of "no pain, no gain"—which has likewise become a mantra of sorts and runs parallel to survival of the fittest.

So as we encountered yoga, we were these competitive corporate types and long-distance runners. We start taking these yoga classes and we are told to be nonjudgmental toward ourselves and others, to not compare ourselves, to allow ourselves to go with the flow and soften into our practice and breathe into a deeper expression of the pose. REALLY? What is all this?

We really tried to apply the *no pain, no gain* approach to yoga, but it simply did not fit. In fact, as we learned to apply a yogic approach instead—allowing our bodies and minds to soften into a posture—we realized that the teacher was indeed right! It became evident with more and more practice that, although it seemed contrarian to our personalities, a non-judgmental, no-expectation, present-moment-awareness approach was far more beneficial. We even developed our own mantras: "Feel your way in; don't force your way in," and "If it hurts, hurting it more will not make it hurt less."

As this yogic philosophy of non-this-or-that took hold with us, we even looked at how that applied in our lives off the mat. Honestly, we have found with our own experiences that a *no pain, no gain* attitude is not a winning proposition and is not sustainable in the long haul. We also noticed that cooperation was a more successful and sustainable business model.

Perhaps it's no surprise that the Yoga Sutras would apply here. Of course! The principle of Ahimsa is where it's at. Just a note about Sanskrit: Be careful to include the "a," as *himsa* means to harm, *ahimsa* means not to. A's are very important in Sanskrit.

HONOR YOUR BODY

Have you ever had an injury or felt tired or out of breath during a physical activity and simply pushed harder, maybe pushing to the point of injury? We have. Usually it does not end well. This doesn't mean that we never take ourselves deeper into an experience or pursue an advanced posture. Going deeper and advancing is a matter of honesty with yourself, a matter of assessing your ego, observing your attitude, and noticing your intention. *Ahimsa* as it applies to you as the practitioner is that you honor your body. Stay within your range of healthy sensation and realistic movement ability.

> *Dennis*: We have been subscribing to Yoga Journal for many years. In our early days of practicing, I felt I had to be just like the models on the cover or in the articles. I thought they were right in their poses and I was wrong, and that I needed to really work much harder to achieve the same expressions or shapes of various poses. For several years I would try to coerce my body to look like the models. Well, if this isn't building a false expectation based on the wrong assumptions, I don't know what is! Needless to say, I was missing the mark, and my practice was frustrating at times.

In retrospect I am pleased that my frustration did not result in my simply quitting yoga altogether. But I am not a quitter. Thankfully, I would learn much later that my body has limitations that cannot be altered with more practice or hard work. In fact, all of us have such limitations. These limits are known as bones!

Even small differences in the geometry of our bones result in large differences in our experience of a yoga pose in comparison to a photo in a magazine. Let's not forget that the models in yoga magazines are selected carefully and then choose poses to model which are ideal for their bodies. This is an interesting parallel to the fashion industry when you think about it.

From the physical perspective, yoga is like any other athletic endeavor or sport. Those who practice and compete at the highest levels are born with anatomies that suit the activity or sport. They are structurally optimal for the activity. Just look at runners, for example.

My realization and liberation came from time spent with Paul Grilley. Kathy and I made one of our most intelligent yoga decisions when we took an anatomy immersion with Paul. He had a set of cadaver bones which he used to illustrate the differences and variations between each skeleton, and also used attendees to show how those small variations limit or allow for range of motion in a multitude of yoga postures. It was amazing and enlightening. He also introduced us to Yin Yoga, which would later become one of our specialties. Truly, his teaching was one of our most memorable and transformative learning experiences. We highly recommend him or at least his video series.

MANAGE YOUR EGO

Only in our minds do we time travel. Through memories, we bring the past to the present. Through expectations, we bring the future to the now. But neither is real! The only thing real is the present moment. Remember, we take in data through our senses, then categorize it into likes or dislikes, which lead to feelings which lead to judgements—and, when repeated, these become habits. And this isn't just true of data from the outside world! Our inner data works the same way.

To truly listen to the signals our bodies are sending requires us to manage our egos. The ego wants you to push yourself, go with that no *pain, no gain* approach. Our ego does not care for truth or limits; the ego wants control over all. Our ego is a master storyteller and loves to compare, compete, and control. *Especially* control. Submission is not a natural part of the ego. But remember, the ego is part of the mind, not the brain or the body. It's not a physiological part of us; it's part of our psychology. It exists as a mental construct, not a physical, chemical, or electrical direct connection to the brain. It does, however, still affect the brain and body via our psycho-energetic and psycho-physical experiences.

Initially, listening to your physical body is all about injury prevention. But eventually—and here is the issue we all face later in life—it becomes a matter of aging gracefully or not.

If it hurts, hurting it more will not make it hurt less. Take this one to the bank!

THE EDGE

This discussion takes us into the concept of what is arguably one of the most important concepts of yoga practice, the "edge." This term is analogous to the edge of a cliff. One more step forward and there you go, falling into certain injury. Staying short of the edge is safe, but limits your experience to see the full view. So the idea of an edge in yoga means the edge of physical injury or psychological discomfort, such as lack of confidence.

The edge has always been with us and is always present, but until we encountered yoga our awareness and relationship to it was virtually unknown. Perhaps the best writing on this subject is by Erich Schiffman in his book, *Yoga: The Spirit and Practice of Moving into Stillness* (Pocket Books, 1997), which is one of our go-to references. We mentioned him earlier when talking about a home practice and his Freedom Style Yoga. We highly recommend his book; frankly, in our opinion, it should be in the personal collection of every yoga teacher.

The edge manifests physically, mentally, and/or emotionally as a result of the entry into a yoga posture or the expression/achievement of a posture. The "and/or" here is key, as one, two, or all three qualities of the edge can manifest.

Let's consider the physical edge first, as it is most tangible. The physical edge represents an invisible yet clear boundary defined by a sensation within a certain area or tissue in the body. It is the first place within the body where you feel the pose—sort of the weakest link within the full anatomy—which is speaking to you through sensation. Generally there is an initial signal or feeling while entering the shape, and then a continuation while holding the pose.

Sensation is the key word when considering a physical edge. The range of sensation goes from none at all up to very painful. Here is the challenging part: Pain is very personal, and what we find painful is totally different for someone else. There are some people who have very high thresholds of pain and must be even more careful not to pass through their edge, resulting in injury.

> *Kathy*: Apparently I have a high tolerance for pain. I found this out after having several procedures done at doctor's offices where the doc would say, *This is going to hurt*, and I basically felt nothing. I soon realized how this high tolerance would come into play in my yoga practice. One day, I was taking a class from one of our favorite teachers and we were all in a wide-leg forward fold sitting on the floor. My body was feeling really good and the teacher was giving us plenty of time to hang out in the shape. I was using my inhale to extend my long torso and the exhale to move deeper. With each breath like this, I felt amazing…until I heard and felt, at the same time, one of my hamstrings pop. Whoa!
>
> At that moment I realized that I had gone too far, way too far, but my body hadn't been sending me what I call "real pain" signals. Of course, it took more than six months to heal my hamstring. I have heard that this particular injury is called "the tear of a thousand tears"

because once you do it, you will likely tear it over and over again.

Because of this, I had to train my mind to back off before I felt pain so I don't injure myself again. This took a while to do. You have to really pay attention to the signals you are getting from your body. Is it discomfort or real pain? Moving into the postures slowly helps, so you have time to detect when you need to stop and not go any deeper. In my body, I now know that this will need to occur before I get the pain signal. We instruct our students to find the sensation somewhere between "boring" and "excruciating." I know that's a wide gap, but it's such an individual thing and every yogi needs to identify their own edge.

Those who are new to yoga are generally unaware of even the physical edge, so this is a new area that must be introduced by an experienced teacher. Awareness of the edge requires a taste of truthfulness and contentment. Staying within a safe range of the edge, yet within a zone of healthy sensation, takes practice.

Now consider the non-physical aspects of the edge. An edge can manifest emotionally and/or mentally. We store negative energies in our bodies. Perhaps these are past traumas, fears, or frustrations. Likewise, energy channels or meridians may be stagnant or blocked, therefore limiting the free flow of prana or chi. The compression, tension, twisting, and shearing (meaning tissues being moved in two opposing directions) actions on our tissues in a yoga pose can trigger a release of thoughts, feelings, and emotions even before the physical edge appears. This is very common particularly in deep hip openers.

So we have these three aspects of the edge: physical, mental, and emotional. But there's more! It's important to note that our edge yields with time. As you hold a posture in a sensation of intensity—whether physical, emotional, or mental—it will yield, allowing for a slightly deeper expression. As long as you don't push, this is safe. In terms of the non-physical edge experience, as we release emotionally and mentally, that edge will yield as well.

> *Dennis*: Experiencing an emotional release can be surprising when it first arises. I have two examples. The first is perhaps unusual, but if I hold a really deep lizard/dragon pose or yogic squat for a long time, even as part of a Yin Yoga practice, I often feel a grin develop on my face and even a little chuckle or laugh on occasion. Weird, right?
>
> Another time I felt a wave of emotion overtake me was at about the mid-way point of a strong power vinyasa practice during an immersion workshop with Baron Baptiste. There was something about that environment—the sequencing, heat, and intensity—that gathered into a perfect storm and I found myself wiping tears from my eyes. There was no underlying reason, feeling, or emotion that I could identify at the time. Sometimes an emotional response just happens, and that's okay. It's not always ours to know why. The key is to allow and observe; see if there is a message or something revealed via the release. Or it could simply be an energetic detox. If you have not had an emotional release yet, keep practicing. Someday you will.

Emotions are just as much a part of yoga as breathing. It's all energy and it's all connected. We hold emotions within various tissues of the body.

Yoga taps into these areas through various postures and use of breath in such a way that clinched or tight tissues soften and release. Sometimes that release carries an emotional element with it and hence we might giggle, laugh, tear up, or cry. This is simply human. But yoga has this uncanny way of tapping into these emotions and letting them release. It's one way in which yoga is a healing modality.

BEYOND ASANA:
THE 5 E'S OF YOGA PRACTICE

Yoga has come a long way in the US since its first introduction by Swami Vivekananda in 1893 and the first studio opening in 1947. Both of these events were the tip of the spear for yoga in America. Later in the 20th century, yoga gained traction as celebrities including George Harrison, Madonna, and Sting become iconic practitioners of this ancient art and science.

Yoga in America, a market survey co-published by Yoga Journal and Yoga Alliance, is a comprehensive assessment of the yoga industry in the US. Its most recent (at the time of this book) findings indicate that between 2012 and 2017, the number of yoga practitioners has increased by fifty percent to over 36 million, while annual practitioner spending grew from $10 billion to $16 billion. That's explosive growth, to say the least.

It's also interesting to note that social media began in the late 90s. Facebook was established in 2004, becoming a publicly traded company in 2012. Instagram was established in 2010 and became a part of Facebook as it went public. In the early 2000s, we saw other social media giants emerge, including Twitter and LinkedIn.

Running alongside the advent of social media came the introduction of the first real camera phone, produced by Sharp Corporation and released in Japan by J-Phone (now SoftBank Mobile) in 2000. It's not a stretch (pun intended) to consider that these advancements in technology helped support this explosive growth of yoga, as more and more students and teachers share their experiences online.

Today, there are at least forty styles of yoga (and growing), so there is a yoga style or type for everyone and almost anything. People have asked us what our style of yoga is—like the world needs another? As full-time yoga teachers, we have traveled extensively and been to numerous studios and retreats and therefore have practiced many styles…and all have something to offer.

Through all this experience and training, we developed over time the concept of the five E's of yoga as key aspects within our practices.

The five E's are:

1. Experiment
2. Experience
3. Embrace
4. Express
5. Empower

We have found that it is the blended combination of these that activates and enlivens yoga in you.

1. Experiment

When a new student first enters a class, it can seem a bit awkward. A yoga class is so different from other fitness classes, especially if it's in a studio rather than a gym. A studio tends to be more authentic, without the limitations that are often placed on a yoga teacher by a gym or resort.

That's not to say these venues are bad; they're just different. It's common that the limitations on the teacher results in a yoga practice that's more like calisthenics, without the deeper aspects that yoga offers. Even so, gym or resort yoga can be a great way to test the waters. After all, our very first class was at a resort!

For a first timer, everything about a yoga practice is different or even strange, from beginning to end: the barefoot thing, the use of a mat and props, different music, sometimes the burning of incense, maybe the suggestion to be quiet before class starts, low lighting or even candlelight, orientation, poses, transitions, breath, the language (Sanskrit), Savasana (the resting pose at the end)…and then there is the Om.

This first E, Experiment, is a methodical process to make a discovery, and the yoga practice is the process by which we make discoveries about ourselves. By definition, experimentation is about openness through observation within a controlled environment within a specified context. In the case of yoga, this refers to the observation of the observer, which is you. The environment is the studio and your yoga mat. The context is presented by the teacher as to how you are guided through poses and transitions with breath.

Yoga will reveal aspects of your breath and body that you never knew. As the practice progresses, you will discover physical strengths and weaknesses, blockages and openings. However, be ready, as the discoveries go beyond the physical aspects of yourself. You will touch the subtle aspects, qualities, and energies of yourself. The discoveries will come in various forms: physical sensations (even pain); an emotion such as frustration; a recollection of an angry or aggressive interaction; remembrance of a lost loved one. These deeper discoveries come with time and practice and will emerge even when you are off the mat, as if there is a residual momentum to the practice that continues far beyond your time on the mat.

2. Experience

With continued practice, experience and knowledge are gained. Pattabhi Jois said, *Practice, practice, practice!* Likewise, we say, *Experience, experience, experience!*

There is power in repetition. What we practice we get better at. However, the *how* and *what* you are practicing is very important. Practicing just to "check the box" is not valid. That's bad practice, and to repeat it is to get better at bad practice!

Beginners and those relatively new to yoga—say, less than a year of classes—need to be very plugged into the basics. In this stage, there is more attention on the physical edges of sensation within the body so as to avoid injury. After a year or so, the yoga practitioner can expand and allow their inner guidance to take over during basic poses and sequences so that these become truly mindful moving meditations. Then, further along, the practitioner can take on more advanced poses, transitions ,and sequences if they are interested. Trying various new things challenges our boundaries and stretches our perceived limitations.

We encounter both physical and psychological edges as we continue the yoga practice. It takes time to develop the experience to assess and know the nature of these edges and then learn how to manage and develop edge awareness as useful tools. In all of our years of trying various fitness forms, it's only through yoga that this awareness of both the physical and psychological edges are emphasized while also honoring our bodies.

3. Embrace

To love others we must love ourselves first.

In today's world this is an elusive concept. Even if we start yoga simply for fitness or as cross-training, more likely than not it evolves into more.

It reveals an inner view through which we can face ourselves. Eventually, at some point in our lives, we do. That is to say, whether in the gym, or in everyday life, we get glimpses of inner aspects of ourselves. Some are deeper and even darker places within us, some are within the body, some are within the subconscious mind. These archived thoughts, feelings, and emotions can act as anchors which limit our abilities and gifts, and can taint self-love and the love of others.

We all have our shades of grey and darkness, but through contemplative practices, like yoga, we observe and acquaint ourselves with these aspects. And as we acquaint ourselves we begin to understand how to grow from within. It's through this deeper place, this understanding, that our hidden abilities, gifts, and self-love emerge and strengthen, allowing us to truly love others. For some, unfortunately, such insights will not come until the ultimate end, during the last breath taken, and this is when deeper regrets are realized. But it's never too late to start.

We are all perfectly imperfect. We all have our gifts and we all have our issues. We all come to the mat with our bad backs, hurting hips or shoulders or knees, past surgeries, traumas, aching hearts, bad attitudes, glass-half-full or half-empty perspectives. We come as we are, flaws and all. Know that yoga is helpful in all these situations and can even be the cure if you let it.

We believe that we are here—that all of humanity is here on this earth—to live, love, learn, and serve. And not just to live, but to be alive in the moment. To love others as we would want to be loved. To learn so as to improve our relationships with the world and better serve. Living and learning go hand-in-hand and feed our ability to love and serve.

To embrace the yoga practice is to integrate acceptance, willingness, and enthusiasm while both on the mat and off. It means we notice our habits and patterns, observe our nature, and are willing to assess and adjust.

It's also important to cut yourself a break and not be so judgmental of yourself. Remember, you are human, and part of the human experience is making mistakes or being mistaken. We all do it. The key to progress and growth is observation with truthful assessment, acknowledgment, and then re-alignment.

It starts on the mat. For example, we might try to insist on getting into a pose at the risk of injury. We might attempt an advanced arm balance, feeling that it is a "must" that day, even though we know we're having a low energy day. *Embracing* within our practice is to balance our edges with our truth. Practicing in this way adjusts our patterns, which changes neural pathways and leads to changes in how we deal with situations off the mat. As we manage our experiences and embrace ourselves during yoga practice, we are slowly molding and changing within as we live our everyday lives.

4. Express

Expression is commonly thought of as how we speak. We mean it in a deeper way. To freely express a pose is to take the shape throughout the whole body-mind system, as an energetic signature of your truest self in that moment.

We are as we are in the moment, not as we were yesterday and not as we hope to be tomorrow. Yes, this sounds deep and rhetorical, but if you ponder it you will see how true it is. The more we practice yoga, the more we are familiar with various poses and sequences and with our edges, then the more we take our selves into a mindful meditative state of flow, a body-mind state in which we practice with no judgement or inhibition.

This is very powerful because of its dynamic somatic awareness. *Soma* is Greek for "the body." Somatic awareness is developed as we practice asana and feel the internal sensations that we experience in the poses, the process of learning to feel your body. This is our internal guidance system. In a vinyasa yoga practice where we flow pose to pose via transitions, we can tap into our inner sensations for guidance, alignment, and expression.

Somatic awareness can be achieved in the simplest of poses and sequences, and yet it's advanced. During a dynamic flow such as Surya Namaskar, it's like a dance, like music. The body-mind system flows and floats upon the breath. Or within a pose such as Triangle, you feel the full energetic expression throughout the whole body—from the fingertips, arms and shoulders, along the spine and legs, with the steady gaze upward and the feet solidly planted energetically into the mat and the earth below.

To *express* is to be in the present moment, locked in and zoned in, with no other concerns. You are sitting (metaphorically) within yourself in equanimity and in balance with all.

5. Empower

This is a big one. The more you practice, the more empowered you become. Yoga is called a practice because you cannot simply read about it or theorize about it to achieve its benefits. You must actually *do* it. The more you do yoga, the more you realize that life itself is also a practice.

This requirement to practice is all about the internalization of yoga as your own experience and expression. You do it yourself. No one can do it for you. No one can experience it for you. No one feels your sensations but you. So yoga is intensely personal; your growth and development in yoga is up to you. You are empowered to make it as you wish or not.

Empowerment on the mat translates to empowerment off the mat. You realize your life experience is up to you. You define your life. You are empowered and are completely responsible for you. No one else is.

•   •   •

These five E's become an integrated blend of your yoga practice and a part of your everyday life.

WHAT IS "ADVANCED YOGA"?

A quick look at posts in social media about yoga reveals an impression that it's just about elaborate, pretzel-like poses. If mastering yoga were about the best pose and the most hits on social media, then any Cirque du Soleil performer, gymnast, or dancer could be a yoga master. Yet this is certainly not the case. Advanced yoga goes beyond asana.

The body and breath, the third and fourth limbs of the eight-limbed path of yoga, are tools used to connect to the body to shift awareness toward self-realization. Unfortunately, most of the work, or tapas in Sanskrit, required for this journey does not lend itself to posts on social media in the hope of going viral. The real work of yoga begins below our surface in the energetic, unseen layers of our being.

Advanced yoga is about enlivening and integrating the yamas and niyamas into our everyday life and placing more emphasis on pranayama, pratyahara, dhyana, and dharana while seeking glimpses of samadhi. The yoga of self-realization is a life-long practice. Integrating the yamas and niyamas is like checking the compass of your life so that you do not veer off course. This takes awareness and discernment. The only way that judgement is involved is in the loving sense of checking our alignment and making the adjustments to be consistent with our inner essence and life purpose.

Advanced practice is about the interior, not the exterior. The body is merely a gateway which requires purification in order to go deeper. Progress is very personal relative to the rate, the depth within each limb, and the degree to which the practice oozes into everyday life. After some time of regular yoga practice, you might find yourself simply appreciating the breeze of wind passing through the trees. Colors might be more brilliant and your gait or posture may reflect a new confidence and poise.

The five E's of yoga can be helpful to look beyond asana during practice and then to begin to integrate yoga within your life off the mat. Experimentation and experience foster an open mind. Embracing and expressing foster allowance and radiance. With empowerment, we take responsibility and stand boldly. As we deepen the practice we are shifting our energetic field, which radiates and touches those around us.

DEMYSTIFYING MEDITATION
AND MINDFULNESS

Even though these terms have become somewhat household phrases over this past decade, they are often confused and misunderstood. One of our missions through our teachings is to demystify meditation and mindfulness, to clarify each independently and both as they relate to one another.

> *Kathy*: There is a wonderful poem by Danna Faulds that begins, "Let me grow so quiet inside that I hear the private conversation of crows as they fly by my window." Can you imagine being that quiet? Is it possible to erase all the noise, all the stuff, all the inner chatter so you can tune into the crows conversing?

Before diving deeper, let's consider some of the myths associated with meditation and mindfulness.

Myth #1: The first thing you need to do to meditate is clear your mind.

No, this is not the case, or even the objective. As we mentioned, we generate between 50,000 and 70,000 thoughts a day! The objective is not to stop our thoughts but to shift our relationship to them. That is, to reduce our engagement with them. In doing so, the volume of thoughts will reduce and therefore so will the mental chatter. Through meditation, we shift our relationship with thoughts and learn their true nature.

Myth #2: It takes too long.

Really, seriously? Do you have just five minutes a day? Since the advent of social media we seem to have plenty of time to check for posts and create our own (social media addiction lends itself to a whole separate discussion…perhaps that will be part of our next book!). Meditation does not take a lot of time.

Myth #3: I don't think I am doing it right.

This is a big one because it's a paradox. Truthfully, there is no right or wrong, per se. There are many methods and techniques, but the good news is you don't have to obsess over the *how*. You simply practice, over and over again. Part of the perception of doing it wrong is loss of focus—which just means you've jumped on the thought train and left the station. When this happens, all you have to do is remember to come back. Perhaps this means simply returning awareness to the breath. So meditation and mindfulness are about remembrance: simply remembering to return to the practice.

Myth #4: Meditation is for special people, like saints, sages, gurus, vegetarians, and weirdos.

Actually, it's *for* anyone and it can *help* everyone. You do not have to go to a cave in Tibet or have a special diet or wear special clothes. You do not have to change your career and move to a new home. It can become your practice of refuge, a practice that makes you a better version of yourself in all aspects of your life. And now meditation and mindfulness are mainstream, as evidenced by the success of books and magazines on the subject and the emergence of meditation studios in major cities.

Myth #5: I need a special place to meditate.

Remember that amazing quote, "Wherever you go, there you are"? Well, wherever you go, your mind is there with you, so you can meditate literally anywhere. We meditate in the car if we arrive at a destination early, in the airport as we wait for a departure, on the plane in flight, and of course on our yoga mat—or more traditionally, on a zafu (a cool cushion made for meditators). You can do it anywhere. It's nice if you have a place in your home that can be made "special," but it's not required.

Myth #6: Meditation conflicts with my religious beliefs.

Actually, pretty much all traditions of religion integrate meditation into their belief systems. Some refer to it as prayer or contemplation. Even the rosary is a form of the ancient Indian tradition of Mantra Japa, which is simply a repetition of a mantra, chant, or prayer as a meditation practice. The use of rosary beads or a mala is simply a mechanical method to keep count and help focus your attention.

Myth #7: It's hard to learn and I need a specially qualified teacher or guru.

Well, once again, no. The key word here is *need*. You can learn to meditate just by sitting quietly and observing your breath. If you want to study or connect within the deeper aspect of a tradition, such as a branch of Buddhism or Transcendental Meditation, then a teacher is helpful as these systems are very sophisticated and rich in tradition and philosophy. Other techniques may require a teacher to guide you to learn the method, but basically, you do not need a teacher to meditate. That's another part of the paradox of meditation: it's actually simple.

Myth #8: I can't do it because I can't sit still.

The good news is, there are many forms of meditation. Some of us prefer to move rather than sit, and for this issue a walking meditation may be a better form. It's okay. Another key point that affects us all is that our minds hate it when we become still while maintaining consciousness. We can sleep and be still, but then we are into our subconscious mental state. The challenge with meditation is managing our interaction with thoughts as they rise and fall *within our consciousness.*

Now that we've looked at the common myths, let's look at what these two things are. Meditation and mindfulness have similarities but are often confused as being the same. Both are of ancient origin and they both deal with management of the mind, but they are, in fact, different. *Meditation* refers to self-regulation or voluntary control practices that focus on improving awareness and attention. The practices are voluntary because we *choose* to meditate, on purpose, and we choose what method to follow.

Meditation starts as concentration. Then as concentration improves, it transitions into meditation. Meditation is an exercise of focus and control. It forms the foundation to enhance your ability to live mindfully with present-moment awareness. Think of meditation as the exercise you do that strengthens your mindfulness or meditative lifestyle.

There are many meditation techniques and methods. Arguably the simplest is placing your awareness upon your breath while sitting in a comfortable seated position. Some methods are very elaborate, but meditation does not have to be complicated. In fact, it's not a practice of doing; it's a practice of being.

Mindfulness is about being present in the present moment as you allow life to flow by—or through—you with no judgement or expectation. It's a practice that can become a part of your life activities. This is a key point of departure from meditation. Consider driving your car. You can be *mindful* as you drive, completely focused and in the flow of the driving process while experiencing no mental chatter or interruptions, but you cannot and should not meditate while driving. You can, however, say you are driving meditatively!

Meditation and mindfulness are like two sides of the same coin. The way to integrate both into your life might be to start with a seated five-minute practice in the morning each day. This could be a simple breath awareness meditation in which you quietly observe your breath for just five minutes. Then, throughout your day, you choose to be mindful in various tasks or experiences. Perhaps you work on active listening, in which you give full attention to the speaker. Or as you do the dishes, you place your entire attention into the process of washing.

So meditation is the tool that sharpens our ability to live with mindful awareness and is used to improve our general wellbeing. It has therapeutic benefits for stress reduction, PTSD, heart disease, trauma, and addiction recovery. Over time and with practice, we feel the benefits of both of these practices physically, mentally, emotionally and energetically, and that shifts our consciousness.

MEDITATION AS A PRACTICE

"Meditation is not a means to an end.
It is both the means and the end."
— *Krishnamurti*

This quote by Krishnamurti captures it concisely. We all want to be happy and healthy, so if that is the end game, then the means to get there is via an intentional path guided by meditation.

In the *Nature of the Mind* section in Foundations, we discussed how the mind works from our interpretation and yogic perspective. Now, let's elaborate upon both meditation and mindfulness for mental management with several simple methods for everyday living.

When it comes to meditation, Patanjali in the Yoga Sutras lays out a progression that really makes sense. *Meditation* refers to *mental practices that focus and train our awareness and consciousness through various methods of self-regulation.* The Yoga Sutras do not specify methods of meditation but rather discuss the challenges we all face. The really good news is that meditation as a practice is simple. The bad news, or shall we say, the challenge, is to practice on a regular basis.

There are several fabulous resources available on the benefits, philosophies, and practices of meditation. This is not a book specifically or solely on meditation, but it is a book to present the importance and accessibility of meditation. What we want to do here is share our perspective on how to bring meditation into your life.

Researchers and practitioners confirm that just a short session each day is enough to make a difference and to reap the benefits of meditation. So as we asked above, don't you have just five minutes to invest in your mind?

Let's ease our way into developing a daily meditation practice.

CONCENTRATION LEADS TO MEDITATION

It starts with concentration. As the definition says, meditation is self-regulation. We have to concentrate first, before we achieve a continuous "flow" within a meditative state. Just like the saying, "You must first walk before you run," the same is true with meditation, but in this case it's all occurring within your mind and not in the physical body. Concentrate, then meditate.

Many teachers and students of meditation miss the point that we all start as beginners with concentration. It's a step-wise approach. The amount of time in concentration shortens as a practitioner's ability progresses. As teachers, we think this is the source of difficulty for many beginners: people think that if they are concentrating, they are doing it wrong. In fact, you *have* to focus/concentrate and follow a meditation method *first*. Only then does the experience transition into a meditative state.

The focal point of your concentration in meditation practices is called *the anchor of awareness*. Each method has its own anchor or focal point. For example, the anchor could be your breath, your movements or posture, or even your feet as you walk. The anchor of awareness is what keeps your mind occupied, thereby distracting you from engagement with your thoughts.

If you are using the breath as a focal point, you can see how, first, you have to collapse awareness onto the breath and maintain it. This takes concentration, as your thoughts keep trying to interrupt your attention. In the beginning, it's helpful to gauge yourself by how long you can keep your awareness on your anchor. As you progress, the amount of time becomes less important, and you find yourself in a different zone, one in which there is disengagement with thoughts. Before you know it, you will say, OMG, I'm meditating!

There will be times when you will drift into a thought or series of thoughts. Well, no worries; just remember to come back to the anchor of awareness. Beginners confuse this as failing at meditation. The truth is, all meditators, even the most advanced practitioners, will drift away. What makes them advanced? They remember to return with no judgement or criticism.

A FEW MEDITATION METHODS:

1. **Breath awareness**: Breath is foundational in virtually all meditation and contemplative traditions. Our breath is our best and most tangible asset in addition to our body. Simply sitting and observing your breath is an excellent meditation method. Notice the nuances of its entry and exit, feel the volumetric change of your body as breath flows through you, perhaps even feel the gentle breeze as breath passes through your nostrils. These are some of the elements of breath awareness that make it such an awesome anchor. And it's in the present moment; you live and breathe in the present moment!

2. **Candle gazing**: Ever notice how everyone is drawn to stare at a campfire or fireplace? Well, that's the basis for candle gazing. Holding a steady gaze on a fire for a period of time is meditation. Using a candle is ideal because we are naturally drawn to the flicker of the flame. See if you can really focus on the flame, paying close attention

to it. This method is also useful because among all of our five senses, our eyes take in the most information: over ten million bits of data per second. Wow! That's a lot of data! Therefore, by this alone, you can see how much of our thinking is driven by our vision. (As a side bar, this is why having a steady gaze—or *drishti* in Sanskrit—is so important in the yoga practice.)

3. **Guided meditations**: These are incredibly useful as they keep you anchored on the verbal guidance along the way.

4. **Walking meditation**: Also quite useful because you can practice noticing, with extreme focus, your surroundings and your movements.

5. **Standing Meditation**: This is one of the earliest forms of meditation and is perfect for anyone who has trouble in a seated posture. And it's harder to fall asleep when you are standing!

6. **Yoga, Tai Chi, or Qi Gong**: All perfect forms of meditation as well!

These are just a few of the many forms of meditation. There are countless variations. They each have an anchor of awareness and each provides a unique meditative experience. It's important to experiment and experience several as you search for the right fit for you. We are each uniquely different so, naturally, no one size of meditation fits all.

TYPES OF LEARNING AND HOW THEY IMPACT YOUR MEDITATION METHOD

With the wide range of meditation styles and methods, we have found that it's helpful to consider an individual's learning style as a basis to choose a starting place. The three learning styles that fit within the context of meditation are visual, auditory, and kinesthetic.

Let's take each one separately.

1. Visual or spacial learners:

These types of learners prefer information presented in pictures, charts, or diagrams. They like things to be orderly and can tell when something is out of alignment. Compatible meditation techniques might be:

- Candle gazing
- Mandala meditation (fixing the gaze on a mandala or sacred image)
- Internal visualization, such as guided imagery or chakra meditations

2. Auditory learners:

These learners prefer to hear information, so they would rather listen than read. Those who have an ear for music or can easily learn a foreign language are often auditory learners. Compatible methods of meditating might be:

- Repeating affirmations, mantras, or prayers verbally or silently
- Chanting or singing
- Guided meditations
- Listening to meditative music, sounds, or vibrations

3. Kinesthetic learners

Kinesthetic folks process information through hands-on experience; actually doing the activity is better than reading about it. These learners are also the ones who can't sit still. For them:

- Yoga, Tai Chi, Qi Gong, walking meditations, chi running
- Expressive dance or movement
- Labyrinth walking

Dennis: Our minds prefer that we move. It's easier to calm the mind with the body in motion. When the body gets still, the mind gets noisy; the monkeys—or, in my case, the entire zoo—goes wild! For this reason, moving meditation is very helpful for everyone, not just the obvious kinesthetic learner. The innate desire to move is why a practice like Yin Yoga, with its long, stationary holds and seated meditations, is so challenging.

Looking at our own learning style is a nice way to select a beginning meditation practice. We encourage you to experiment! After some time, you might wish to try some of the other methods or even pursue meditation practices within a tradition like Zen or Tibetan Buddhism.

THERE IS AN APP FOR THAT!

Of *course* there is an app for meditation! Many, in fact!

Dennis: I was very resistant in the beginning, until a weekend immersion several years ago when a student said, "Consider the app as a contemporary form of mala beads, but with much more capability." So I tried it. Not only did I become a fan, but now we are providers of guided meditations for Insight Timer, a popular meditation app.

An app can be very helpful for some folks who have difficulty with a routine meditation practice. Meditation apps are not just timers; they also provide a wide range of meditation styles from guided meditations to meditative instrumental music. They track your progress and you can set reminders. We highly recommend apps.

MINDFULNESS IN EVERYDAY LIFE

Becoming more mindful during the day is the result of progressive practice. Concentration leads to meditation. Meditation is the foundation—the mental workout, you might say—which leads to living your life meditatively or mindfully. Meditativeness and mindfulness are states of being or living. Again, this is simple *conceptually* but difficult in practice, as we are continuously bombarded by our thoughts.

Active listening is another form of mindfulness. Can you truly be present in a discussion without checking your smart phone or tuning into other nearby conversations? Can you focus on the speaker and listen to each word? Can you listen without thinking about what you are going to say next? Sometimes we get so caught up in our response or trying to one-up the story that we miss what is really being said.

> *Dennis:* I have found that even if I think of a similar situation in my life while someone is recounting their story, I don't always have to share it. Many times, my story dilutes what the other person is telling me, so it's occasionally best to refrain and let them have their say. Being an active listener is one key to success and is a means of paying respect to the speaker.

We all drift from mindfulness. In fact, we are more mindless than mindful. As we like to say, there are times when you have to be a bit ridiculous with yourself and apply what we refer to as the three W's.

Here is how it works: During those times in which you realize you are unplugged and have drifted off course, ask yourself:

What am I doing right now?
Where am I?
When am I doing it?

Yes, these are rhetorical as the answers are obvious: I am doing this, here, right now. You are reading this, wherever you are, right now! But these questions will help ground you back in mindfulness.

FINAL THOUGHTS

Meditation and mindfulness are indeed the secret sauces to success, health, happiness, and wellbeing. Take some time for yourself, experiment, and have a sense of humor. Remember, everything matters.

INGESTION:
IT'S MORE THAN JUST FOOD

As we have already discussed, our perceptions are directly linked to and fed by our senses. We receive input from the external world through the senses, this input is processed and assimilated, and then it becomes a part of our being. Now consider ingestion. The obvious example is the food we eat, which is ingested through the mouth and hopefully enjoyed via taste, texture, and smell. After ingestion, food is processed via our digestive system, nutrients are absorbed, and, eventually, waste is expelled. But what about ingestion via the other senses?

From an Ayurvedic viewpoint (the science of life, which is a sister science to yoga), the body is a vessel which defines a boundary between the interior and exterior. The five senses—hearing, touch, vision, taste, and smell—interact with the five elements—ether, air, fire, water, and earth. These elements are the manifested external world and are perceived through the senses. Taking this view, the five senses are the gateway from the exterior to the interior of ourselves on the physical, mental, and emotional levels.

As an analogy, consider the five senses in the context of data from the IT world. Again, via a Google search, "ingestion" is defined as *obtaining data for use and/or storage into a data base.* We can look at sounds, vibrations, smells, the way things feel to our touch, and tastes as data. Why not? With this view, all information (or, let us say, all energy) we take in and ingest is then used (digested) or stored in a database (mind) for future use.

Combining the Ayurvedic and IT views, ingestion is the intake of information, food, or energy for immediate use, such as offsetting hunger pains, conversational dialog, or perhaps the simple enjoyment of listening to classical music or smelling a rose. Sight, sound, taste, smell, and touch also feed our memories, thoughts, and intellect for future use. Our bodies are miraculous vessels, able to ingest energies from multiple sources. Therefore, what we ingest is very important as it becomes us!

We already know it's important to eat wisely, to eat healthy nourishing food. Isn't it, then, equally important to be selective of what comes in via the other senses? You may ask, how do we feed our other senses? It's easy; we do it constantly! In fact, we are taking in sensory data with every moment. It's a constant flow, and certainly way more than the equivalent of just three meals per day. You are doing it right now!

We are bombarded with sensory input from all sources and directions. Everything you take in via all five senses becomes a part of you on a physical, mental, emotional, and energetic level—for better or worse. As practicing yogis, we observe ourselves and assess our experiences. And so it is with our concept of ingestion. What we allow to enter our vessel, our body-mind system, literally becomes a part of our being. Whether it's the food we eat or sounds and sights, these impressions are ingested and digested. Especially if repeated over and over.

Consider *how* you eat dinner. How mindful is your dining? Are you enjoying your food through all your senses, noticing taste, texture, and aroma? Do you ever multi-task, wolfing down dinner while texting, working, or checking your email? Do you typically watch TV while eating? Seemingly innocuous, TV has a real effect on your digestion and future thoughts, emotions, and impressions. Eating while watching the evening news, for example, not only fills your mind with negative thoughts, sounds, and images, but also leaves impressions that stay with you. Even if your food has all the right labels—organic, free range, shade grown, gluten-free, lactose-free, sugar-free, etc.—the energetic negative overflow of the news outweighs the good food labels and will dramatically affect digestion.

Take the news issue deeper and let's look at it separately from eating a meal. Whether on TV, radio, or your favorite webpage, the news is mostly negative. Rarely do you see a positive, heartwarming news piece. Why? Because negative news sells!

We live in a culture and are a species that is obsessed with negative news. We are not saying you should take on the approach of the ostrich who sticks his head in the sand. On the contrary! We are all far too aware of war, conflict, religious persecution, racism, discrimination, civil rights issues, and other atrocities that exist in the world. Simply by being alive in this world, via osmosis, we are exposed to such news. And simply by exposure to negative images, sounds, and thoughts, we are physiologically and psychologically affected. Remember, negative sticks to our minds like velcro. Our hormones shift toward fight or flight, cortisol increases, we have short-tempered reactions, and negative memories arise.

So what can we do? To paraphrase Mahatma Gandhi, "Be the change that you want to see in the world." The best way to create change in the world is to change yourself. Stay positive in your own sphere of influence; be an example of compassion and loving-kindness. We seemingly cannot solve world hunger on our own, but we can take personal steps and make changes in our relationship with food that will impact world hunger in a positive way. The same is true with discrimination. First, look inside. Become indiscriminate in your relationships and this will expand by way of example to others.

Excessive negative bias is a major issue. In some way, it's not our fault (arguably, it comes to us as humans by way of our nature), but it is very manageable. The key is to recognize the symptoms, like you would for any illness or disease. Recognition, followed by awareness with the right actions, leads to wellness and happiness.

> *Kathy*: We have a rule at our house and ask (politely) that our guests try and honor it. During mealtimes, no cell phones, iPads, or other electronic devices allowed. Even if something comes up in conversation and someone gets the urge to Google it, we try to refrain. Just to go off on a little tangent here, there is such a thing as the Google Effect. If we continually rely on looking up facts on the internet instead of trying to recall them, we lose the ability over time to retain that info. Plus, it dampens our creativity. So the next time you want to Google it, take a few minutes to try and recall that info from your own brain instead. It will help you recall it again in the future as well.

> *Dennis*: I must admit, I am a recovering CNN junkie. Any network news that covered national and international conflicts or news related to governmental funding for military products was my preferred drug as I was in that profession. Over the years this became an addiction. When I was traveling, the first thing I would do when entering a hotel room would be to turn on the news. That was bad enough, but even when traveling

on vacation with Kathy I would do the same. While at home, I drove her crazy with my constant need to check in on the news.

I could not see the effect it was having within myself as I was in the middle of the experience. I could not see the forest for the trees, as they say. Honestly, being a news junkie is like any other addiction with respect to the need for rehab. Although mine was not as devastating as, say, drug addiction, it had characteristics that were. It filled me with disturbing information and terrible images, and it was burdensome. It had a negative effect on those around me, especially Kathy. Yes, I was up on all the latest and yes, it served my career very well. However, over time, the ugly head of this addiction became evident and I had to address it.

Thankfully, I had found yoga and meditation. Yoga is about relationships on all levels and types. I had an obsessive relationship with the news that I had to shift. Through diligent practice, mindful awareness, acceptance, truthfulness, and adjustment over time, the hold of the news softened its grip on me and eventually my habit shifted. For me today, the news is a resource which I tap into carefully, occasionally, and only for specific information.

FOOD BECOMES YOU

Following this same logic, we must look at our ingestion of actual food itself with an equally critical eye. What we eat becomes us. Literally, on a cellular level, our food merges within us as nutrients, toxins, or waste.

Inorganic food is defined as any food that has utilized synthetic products, such as chemical fertilizers and pesticides, in its production. Genetically modified food (GMO) is considered inorganic. Realizing that all is energy, to consume inorganic food is to consume these synthetic products, such as chemical fertilizers, pesticides, and genetic modifications. Is this what we really, consciously want to eat?

Yes, it is true that organic alternatives cost more. No surprise, as to certify and verify organic food takes extra effort and copious detail, ensuring that every ingredient meets the proper specifications. Our local natural foods grocer investigates the supply chain of its suppliers and all their ingredients to be sure, confirming claims, testing, and process compliance. Layers of additional expense are added to cover the extra attention and oversight required to ensure the quality and nutritional value of organic foods. Therefore, of course, they are more expensive.

This happens in part because disclosures and labeling of our food—right along with the whole GMO issue—has become a national political football that the food industry, with their well-funded lobbyists, fights very aggressively. When you dig deeper into the issue of labeling and protecting our food, you find that the US is far behind other countries. Wouldn't it be interesting if the government fully embraced non-GMO labeling and truly enforced compliance? This food industrial lobby is one of the strongest and most highly funded lobbying efforts in DC, but we will not digress.

Now a more difficult subject regarding food. It's clear—or, perhaps, unclear—that most of the general population does not really know anything about the food we eat. With continued population growth, technological advancements, and the sheer pace of our contemporary lifestyles, meals are more like pit stops and real food is more like premium gas. So we tend to go cheap and fast with little or no regard to the consequences.

Knowing our food seems so obvious. But the food industry, including most grocers, have managed to market and reposition food in such a way that we are desensitized and somewhat blinded to the realities of what our food is, where it was sourced, how it was grown or raised, and how it was processed. It takes a fair amount of awareness and willingness to really take the time to read labels in the grocery store before placing food products in the cart. We all lead busy lives, and grocery shopping can sometimes be more like a sprint through the park, but selection and eventual purchase of the food we consume deserves serious thought. If food becomes us, it's extremely important to be careful about our choices. Isn't food our best investment in preventative medicine? Is that the best place to pinch our pennies? We do not think so.

Diet, nutrition, and exercise are perhaps the most debated topics on the planet and the subject of millions of books and blogs. We do not claim to be dietitians and certainly are not nutritionists, but we have tried many diets in our day, gaining and losing weight only to gain it back (with the exception of the last fifteen years), and we have nearly sixty years each on this earth worth of experience. So let's take on the issue of animal-based foods.

Heart disease and cancer are the two leading causes of death in the US, and consumption of animal food products is the leading contributor to both of these. Perhaps the most comprehensive, international, and reviewed study of the relationship between the consumption of animal products and chronic illness is The China Study, by T. Collin Campbell, et al. There are many other studies, articles, and books that validate and support that animal food products are counterproductive to a sustainable, long-term healthy life. A quick Google search of your own will surface more that you might have wanted to know on the subject.

Couple this with the ingestion, digestion, and assimilation of the *effects* of animal slaughter. Remember, what we eat we become. Mass industrialization of the past thirty years or more has changed the nature (pun intended) of more than just the landscape of the farm.

> *Dennis*: Growing up in a small town in Massachusetts and living in the mountains just south of Vermont and New Hampshire, I was born into a hunting and fishing family. I spent a lot of time in the woods, but much of it was with a gun in hand—or a fishing pole, knife, or bow. My father and I would hunt rabbit, pheasant, quail, and deer.
>
> I got my first gun when I was about ten years old. My parents were very strict in my training and use of weapons. Over the years, my guns included handguns, shotguns, and rifles with long-range scopes. This does beg the question of fairness in the "sport" of hunting. With much practice, I became a very good hunter and fisherman. However, even at my so-called best, even with my best shot, almost every victim of my gun was an animal which suffered an excruciating death and finally had to be put out of its misery with my own hands.
>
> The same is true of all the fishing we did. Some weekends we would catch a hundred or more brook trout. Once they were reeled in, some had swallowed the hook and line; they were still alive and gasping and I would have to ease their final pain. I have seen and literally felt in my own hands the suffering of many animals.
>
> Whether by gun, arrow, or hook, I had set the intention to kill! To take the life of another sentient being.

Hunting and fishing back then was done for both sport and consumption. However, that does not justify the killing. When I was about seventeen years old, I had a chance to kill my first deer. Everything up to that point had prepared me for that moment, as a deer was a prize kill. In retrospect, that moment was a sign of a light within me. I raised my gun, took aim with my finger on the trigger. Just as I was about to shoot, a wave of compassion came over me. I could not do it. I saw before me the beauty of this creature and felt an awareness of its family and its innocence. It was soon after that I lost interest in hunting and fishing of any kind. I went on to college and never looked back.

Well, at least not until I found yoga. You see, as we have said many times, yoga is about relationships. It has a way of revealing ourselves to ourselves. As I reflected upon my younger days and upon the killing of innocent animals, my heart broke for the pain and suffering I caused. Think of this, I had dogs and cats as pets. How could I hunt animals but love my pets? Are they all not sentient beings? Yes, of course they are! These lives, the ones that I took, haunt me today as negative memories, negative impressions that became a part of me. This subject hurts me deeply, but I share it openly and honestly as I want to express this publicly, to clarify my personal experience and perhaps use myself as an example so that others might see the same light I saw within.

Animals raised for food live terrible lives and die horrible deaths whether they are free range, organic, or victims of industrialized slaughterhouses.

Even before the "process" begins, animals are traumatized, causing hormonal shifts that create a state of the equivalent of fight or flight throughout their lives. As death approaches this terror increases, changing them on a cellular level. This trauma and hormonal chemical soup merges into their tissues, the flesh which makes its way into grocery stores for eventual consumption. When this flesh is eaten, the negative energies of terror and trauma of all slaughtered animals and fish is ingested, digested, and becomes you. And never mind the addition of growth and reproductive hormones that are pumped into these animals to increase production and decrease manufacturing costs.

It's all energy. In the case of animal products, it's all negative energy of trauma and terror. Do you want to consume this kind of energy? Is it necessary that other beings die horrific lives for us to live? The answer, of course, is no. As vegans for over twelve years, we can absolutely confirm this. We now eat the same diet as gorillas, elephants, and even the extinct brontosaurus. We eat plants! We are stronger, happier, and healthier than ever.

SKIN AND BEAUTY PRODUCTS

Okay, hold those thoughts regarding diet. Now let's consider skin and skin care products. From the perspective of Traditional Chinese Medicine, the skin is the third lung. Western medicine will tell you it's our largest organ. What is applied to the skin is also ingested—known as absorption—as though it's eaten! And here's the kicker: Whatever's applied on our skin does not pass through the liver for filtration and can make its way directly into the bloodstream (Huffington Post, The Blog, 6/2012).

So, our skin should be a key priority and consideration for our long-term health. The same awareness and study of the foods we eat should also be applied to our skin care products. Hence, read labels. Look for organic, natural, non-GMO products.

Kathy: Okay, friends, if you are buying your cosmetics, shampoo, hair products, deodorant, and lotions at the drug store, stop! Or at least reconsider what you are putting on your skin and hair. It's highly likely that they have damaging ingredients. Buy these at the health food store or online after seriously examining what's in them. And don't forget about your laundry soap, dish soap, and cleaning products, as these come in contact with your skin as well. Don't even get me started on sunscreens. Did you know that most of them actually cause skin cancer, the very thing you are trying to prevent? I won't get into that here, but Google it for yourself.

INGESTION AS A SPIRITUAL PRACTICE

As noted above, we define ingestion to include all input through the five senses. However, ingestion is more than just a matter of sensory data input and fueling the machine. We as a society in the 21st century have forgotten that food is a spiritual practice. That what and how we eat is connected to our spirit. Virtually every tradition and every religion in documented history includes rituals, guidelines, and practices around food. In the same way, the practice of ingesting anything becomes spiritual when treated with mindfulness and care.

Ingestion as we present it highlights and emphasizes that *everything matters*. As that famous one-liner says, "You are what you eat." We would modify that to say, "You are what you ingest!" Negative or positive, energy is energy—and it's everywhere, in all things, including your most precious and miraculous body-mind system. Treat your body-mind system as a temple that is spiritually sacred. It's the only one you have in this lifetime.

SOUND, VIBRATION, MUSIC, AND MANTRAS

"If one listens with undivided attention
to the sounds of stringed instruments, he will, in the end,
be absorbed into the ether of Consciousness
and thus attain the nature of Shiva."
Vijnanabhairava, Dharana 18, Verse 41 (Sturgess, 2015)

This verse really says it all. Taken from an ancient text, dating back to 800 CE, this verse reminds us of the wisdom available through sound and vibration. Listening with undivided attention is the key. Focused attention places your awareness upon the sounds as they arrive in the present moment. When we focus with awareness, the notes, chords, and music collectively provide a melodic navigation through our thoughts, feelings, and emotions, relaxing us physiologically via our nervous system.

An alternative translation of the quote above comes from Lorin Rouche in *The Radiance Sutras*. This translation says, "Immerse yourself into the rapture of music, take in each note, each chord." In other words, allow sounds, vibrations, notes, and chords to become you as you assimilate or ingest them.

We did not find this verse until much later in our time with yoga. It was after a dear friend bestowed a sitar to Dennis in December of 2015. Dennis had always felt the six strings of guitar were challenging enough, but try tackling eighteen strings on a sitar!

> *Dennis*: This was not just any sitar. It was owned by a singer-songwriter named Chris, a Kirtan leader and Kundalini yoga teacher who passed unexpectedly. His sister became a yoga student of ours and, more importantly, a dear friend. She surprised us as she presented me with her brother's sitar after a small dinner gathering. She asked that I play it in his memory and continue sharing its vibes. Wow, I was humbled, and what an honor! Soon after my first lesson, I ran into the verse above while surfing the web for sitar guidance. It's become a part of my meditations and often joins my practice sessions for inspiration as I continue to share the vibes in honor of Chris.

The use of sound and vibration, music, and mantras in meditative and contemplative practices dates back to ancient indigenous peoples around the world. Predating documented history, the use of voice and primitive instruments became parts of rituals and practices designed to lead into deeper states of consciousness. Lacking the scientific methods and instruments of today, the ancients of the past could not quantify the effects—but through empirical means they knew that sound, vibration, music, and mantra created positive change.

Yoga emphasizes the connection to sound and vibration. Back in the days of old, gongs, bells, flutes, and drums were used as a means to connect with the body and mind. Music evolved as an aid to facilitate the experience of yoga.

In music, harmony is defined as a combination of notes making up a chord which has a pleasing effect upon the listener. This would imply there is a combination of notes which are not pleasing, an effect that is described as *dissonant* in the realm of music. Pleasing sounds are contrasted by those which are not. Yet both are essential to understanding and feeling each other. Sound familiar?

Well, is this not Yin and Yang? In this musical example, the Yin quality is represented by the harmonious; the Yang quality by the dissonant. You could say there is sonic or acoustic duality at play. From a musical perspective, major chords seem happier than minor chords, which are darker. But both are required to express the full spectrum of emotions in music.

Sound propagates as vibrations through the air and environment around us. The right combination of notes, tempo, dynamics, and silence (yes, silence) creates music. All feed and support each other. Sound, vibration, and the resulting music all are energy.

SOUND AND VIBRATION AS HEALING MODALITIES

We receive acoustic vibrations, sound, and music by more than just our ears. Hearing is just one part of the experience.

For the purpose of simplicity, let's speak of all sound rather than just music, specifically. Sound directly affects the body-mind system. The nature and texture of the sound can result in relaxing, neutral, energetic, or even debilitating effects upon our systems. As sound waves enter the body, they enter as energy, within the audible range of frequencies which we, as humans, can hear. This energy is transmitted into the brain and converted into feelings and sensations.

Have you ever wondered what sound looks like as it travels toward you? We have. Think about times when you are at a live concert or in a room with a loud sound system. Recall feeling the vibrations on your skin? In the late 1600s, a simple experiment demonstrated that each sound or note has a signature pattern that is more than a simple wave traveling through air. Sound travels as a three-dimensional bubble, not just as a wave. The bubble itself is a complex, interwoven structure of sound waves, unique to each sound.

Over the years of study and development, this science became known as Cymatics, the science of visualizing audio frequencies. With Cymatics we now can see sound. The most impressive images and videos are by Nigel Stanford on his website, nigelstanford.com. They are absolutely amazing. Go there and see sound, literally! This site has basic info, beautiful photography, and videos.

Each note and sound has a characteristic pattern. Some might resemble a mandala. With this understanding, we can imagine how these bubbles and patterns enter our ears and touch or massage the surfaces of our skin. There is much debate and speculation about the use of Cymatics as a therapeutic method as there is no doubt that sound does have an effect, positive or negative, upon matter.

A key element of how we as humans convert sound to feelings and sensations is through stimulation of the vagus nerve. This nerve is known as the "wandering nerve" as it starts at the base of the brain, meanders down through the neck, and interfaces with all major organs and glands in the torso. The vagus nerve is responsible for most of our parasympathetic response, also known as the relaxation response.

This wandering nerve has been the subject of many investigations relative to inflammation and stress management (Shaw, November, 2017). Stimulation of the vagus nerve has been shown to improve resistance to strokes and heart attacks, increase calmness and concentration, reduce inflammation, and add to a more positive attitude. These studies are exciting as we can stimulate the vagus nerve for our own health and wellness by very simple means! For example, the vagus nerve is the key means by which sound is converted and transmitted within the body-mind system, and so sound, vibration, singing, and chanting are all avenues to stimulating the vagus nerve.

Even our own voice and breath will activate and stimulate the vagus nerve and, in turn, the parasympathetic nervous system. Our vocal cords and the massage of breathing cause this stimulation. In addition, when we listen to gentle harmonic sounds or meditative music, the vibrations of the notes are transmitted into our nervous and endocrine systems, resulting in a euphoric relaxed state. However, sounds of the opposite quality — such as fingernails scratching a chalk board — do not cause relaxation. It would be of no surprise that sound can be used as either a healing modality or as torture; there has been plenty of research and application in both cases.

Entrainment is another aspect of our human experience of sound. We hear sounds and music, but we also feel the texture and tempo. In fact, we naturally become part of the tempo or beat through the process known as entrainment. *Entrainment* is the synchronization of organisms to an external rhythm, to the beat. Have you ever been in a cafe or club with rhythmic music and notice how people start swaying or tapping their feet in tempo with the music? That's an example of entrainment in the musical sense. This same synchronization occurs on a cellular level as well. Tones, sounds, and vibrations are absorbed within and create resonances with our cells and organs.

There is also brainwave entrainment, in which the brain's frequency response shifts to align to a frequency of a beat. Similarly, as noted above, brain waves can be stimulated by sound or electromagnetic frequencies to pulse or follow vibrational patterns. Sound meditations that include binaural beats—beats that are pulsed with slightly different frequencies into each ear—create a state of entrainment. Many such recordings have been produced by sound therapists and meditative musicians, and they are even available in some free meditation apps.

The sciences of sound, Cymatics, and entrainment are very broad and can be extremely technical. But their applications as healing modalities have only recently been recognized in the medical world. There is so much more to how vibrations affect us. Our point here is a reminder that sound, vibrations, and music affect us on many levels, and being mindful of that is part of both ingestion and a spiritual practice.

As yoga teachers, we like to say we are facilitating an experience. And just as the studio space, flooring, lighting, and scents are important, bowls, bells, gongs, flutes, and other forms of music are key elements of the overall experience as well.

> *Dennis*: They say, "What goes around comes around." Could that be with past academic degrees and studies? I have a Master's degree in Structural Mechanics. My thesis was on sound transmission through partitions and walls. It's crazy how some aspects of your life can come full circle. So here I am—I have not been a practicing engineer for decades but all of my physics, acoustics, and mathematics studies are still serving me well. Not sure my parents see it that way, though!

DIPPING OUR TOES
INTO THE WATERS OF MANTRA

Mantras—words, phrases, or sounds which are repeated for a specific purpose or intention— are very old; ancient, in fact. So old that they predate many languages of the western world. This is especially true of the yogic chants of Vedic origin, which were written in Sanskrit.

Chanting is a form of mantra, and there are many traditions in which chanting is prominent. The word Om, which is said to be the primordial sound of the universe, is a common mantra in yoga. Joining in on the opening or closing Om in a yoga class is where most of us begin to try chanting. At first it seems strange, but as part of a group there is comfort, as you can blend in. A group Om is so powerful as it connects you vocally and energetically. You can feel the vibrations build from within and around you.

Finding—or having a teacher give you—a mantra that resonates with you is the first step in this ancient practice.

> *Dennis*: I recall how taken I was when I first heard the Gayatri mantra. The version I became obsessed with is Deva Premal's from The Essence album. Looking back, it's interesting how the mantra became a part of me. First, I was drawn to learning it line by line. There was something about the texture of the Sanskrit and the tempo of the phrasing. I found myself mentally reciting it over and over. Eventually I would chant it as a closing for some of our yoga classes.

> The Gayatri mantra reminds us of the bigger picture. We are part of something much larger than ourselves. There is something about its ancient origin and organic

connection, its reference to qualities of the sun, and the calling for us all to take on the same qualities and shine them indiscriminately for the benefit of all beings. We will elaborate on this in Appendix 1.

FINDING YOUR VOICE

It's important to know that chanting in yoga is not a performance. In fact, it's the antithesis of performance. We typically come into chanting from the perspective of singing, thinking we have to hit all the notes and be in key. But to focus on that is to miss the point and the essence of chanting. Chanting is not about being in proper key or hitting all the notes. It's about the mantra itself, about the meaning and vibration of the mantra and integrating these within you. It's about *energetic* harmony and resonance, not the harmonies of voice in the context of singing and performing. Now, if you happen to be a singer or have had voice lessons, great! Be thankful for your gift and training. And, even still, be free and just go with it.

Each mantra carries a message and meaning which reveals itself through its vibrations and language. Your uninhibited expression of your voice is how these mantras become more potent. Do not feel pressure to do it right or to sing well. Do not even worry about proper pronunciation. What matters is your intention and awareness of the meaning of the mantra.

> *Dennis*: In my previous corporate life, my responsibilities would require me to speak publicly during my business travels. I had no difficulties speaking in front of relatively large groups, even up to a couple hundred people occasionally.

> Then we ran into yoga and chanting, which brought me to a new realization. I could recite chants and speak

them in front of people, but as soon as I shifted it from speaking to singing, my voice was lost. Literally, it was like my throat closed, not allowing me to continue. My heart rate would increase and this wave of anxiety would wash over me.

I kept practicing but I could not progress. It was after quite some time, as we developed our understanding of chakra theory and psychology, that I realized my issue was, in fact, a throat chakra issue from my childhood.

In my pre-teen years, it became evident that I had a speech impediment. I was mis-pronouncing words with "ch" in them, like church, for example. You can imagine how this worked with my popularity on the playground and during gym class!

It was not a doctor or speech therapist who resolved the mechanical aspects of this. It was my cousin, who showed me I was not enunciating properly. Literally, it was that simple. However, the residual mental trauma of being ridiculed as a child stayed with me, although it did not rear its ugly head until I tried to sing a chant.

Fortunately, because of my study of the chakras, I was able to work on myself via affirmations, meditation, and just plain old practice to heal myself. I balanced my throat chakra and became our own best real-life example of how applying the right methods will release and renew areas of congestion and negative energies.

Kathy: I sang in our church choir growing up as a kid. Not a soloist, mind you, but I could carry a tune in a large group. And I loved it! I can also remember words to songs pretty easily, so I was all for singing chants and learning Sanskrit.

But performing in a choir is nothing like chanting. During choir practice, we had to make sure the sopranos, altos, tenors, and bass singers all sounded good together. Every choir member had music to follow for us to be in key and in perfect harmony. Rehearsal was all about getting the music to sound its very best.

Chanting feels completely different. It doesn't matter if any of us are singing in the same key, are in tune, are with the beat...none of that! And also, in chanting, if you get caught up in the moment and stop singing, it's no big deal.

An excellent way to gain experience with chanting is to download a few of your favorite mantra artists. Today there are many singer songwriters who have arranged and recorded virtually all of the ancient chants. Play their recordings and chant along. This helps you find your voice, develop a connection to the chant, and learn the pronunciation of the chant in its original language. What matters most is having a basic understanding of the meaning of the chant and then internalizing it as you chant. Closing your eyes is best, unless you are driving!

Most of us have lived our entire lives accumulating negative energies, which manifest in our bodies and minds and culminate in pain and suffering. Chanting works to unravel this negative energy, re-wire our brains, and shift our consciousness, leading us toward happiness and wellbeing. As teachers and practitioners, we consider chanting ancient mantras to be one modality among several that, together, form the technology of yoga. It's a powerful tool that's fun and can be done anywhere, anytime, silently or audibly.

THE LANGUAGES OF YOGIC MANTRAS

Our first exposure to Sanskrit came in the first yoga class we attended. We found it captivating, although we had no idea then how relevant and important its use was to the tradition and practice of yoga. Even in our early years, references to Sanskrit added a richness to the poses, breath, and experience. Sanskrit is truly a beautiful language.

As an example, we grew to love the use of the closing word, *namaste.* Loosely translated, it means *the light in me recognizes and bows to the light in you.* A little more meaningful than, say, *Hey, how you doing?*

The Sanskrit language predates organized religion, dating back to 2000 years BCE. This language became the foundation from which many of today's languages are derived. With around fifty letters, Sanskrit is very broad in its range of meanings and use. It is also an energetic language with primordial roots, so it carries an energetic meaning along with the literal one.

The other language of interest from a yogic perspective is Gurmukhi. Gurmukhi means "from the mouth of the guru." This language was derived and developed during the 10th-14th centuries CE. Like Sanskrit, Gurmukhi carries an energetic quantity in addition to the functional meaning. It is the language of Kundalini Yoga and it's an equally beautiful language.

To translate an ancient chant from Sanskrit to English is, of course, possible, but some of the essence is lost along the way. It's easy to image that translations may be approximations, considering that English has only twenty-six letters to the fifty or so in Sanskrit. In addition, the original chant may carry multiple meanings within the original context. Because of this, we like to think of the English translation as a glimpse or shadow of an original meaning which is deeper than can be expressed in English. Certainly you could recite or even sing the English translation of a given chant, but to do so would lose the energetic quality of the original. In its complete form, each yogic chant carries both functional and energetic meanings and qualities.

> *Dennis*: Okay, so here comes a big concern that we have faced, as have many other yoga teachers—that chanting in these languages might somehow change your religion.

> Here's our thought on that. Sanskrit is a language, not a religion. It also predates all organized religions, as we mentioned. Also, Sanskrit fed the development of the Indo-European languages from which English was derived. Chanting in Sanskrit—and for that matter, even practicing yoga—will only change your religion if you let it or want it to.

SANSKRIT, MANTRAS, AND THE CHAKRAS

Here is another amazing point to consider. During our studies, we learned there is an interesting relationship between Sanskrit and the chakras. Each of the seven chakras, based upon the yogic conceptual model, is represented by a symbol which includes a certain number of lotus petals, a mandala, and a bija mantra. A bija mantra is a *seed syllable*, a single sound—or as we like to consider them, an energetic key that unlocks the positive energies and attributes of each chakra center when recited. These layered elements define the energetic qualities of each chakra center.

The number of lotus petals for each chakra symbol corresponds to the number of nadis to which it connects. This is important relative to Sanskrit as the total number of lotus petals in the symbols of the first six chakra centers added together—that is, starting from the base of the spine with the first (Muladhara) chakra, and going up to the sixth (Ajna) chakra—is the same as the number of letters in the Sanskrit alphabet (Sturgess, 2005).

The significance of the petals and letters on the chakra symbols is amazing to consider in terms of chanting mantras in Sanskrit. Why, you may ask? Because when we chant a mantra in Sanskrit with a clear understanding of the mantra, calling in the intention of the mantra, and with a feeling-sense that the mantra has already delivered its purpose within you, we are activating the corresponding petals of the chakras. So as we chant we are enlivening the chakras and the related channels in a very powerful way. Through mantra meditation, we are literally tuning our body-mind systems and our spirits as though we are musical instruments.

JAPA MANTRA AND JAPA MALA: THE POWER OF REPETITION

Japa is the Sanskrit word for repeat or repetition, which is a key element of practice. What we repeat, we improve. The more consistent we are with repetition, the better we become. *Japa Mantra* is a form of meditation practice in which a mantra is repeated, either as an audible whisper or silently in the mind. *Japa Mala* refers to the use of a mala necklace to keep count of the repetitions.

This happens to be one of our favorite forms of meditation. It's very powerful, as it keeps the mind focused. Spoken or sung, repetition of mantras also helps improve your respiration system and stimulate the parasympathetic nervous system. So if you relax and let go into the japa mantra meditation, it's powerful!

The next obvious question is, how many repetitions? There are several different theories on this. We believe in the yogic perspective of connecting the number to the universe by using factors of 108. This could be 3, 9, 18, 27, 54, or, of course, 108.

The number 108 is a very interesting and auspicious number:

- Stonehenge is 108 feet in diameter.
- There are said to be 108 energy lines, or nadis, in the body.
- The distance between the Earth and Sun is 108 times the diameter of the Sun.
- The diameter of the Sun is 108 times the diameter of the Earth.
- The distance between the Earth and Moon is 108 times the diameter of the Moon.
- 108 degrees Fahrenheit is the internal temperature at which the human body's vital organs begin to fail from overheating.
- In astrology, there are 12 houses and 9 planets. 12 times 9 equals 108.
- There are 54 letters in the Sanskrit alphabet. Each has masculine and feminine, also known as shiva and shakti. 54 times 2 is 108.
- There are 108 cards in an Uno deck! Not sure if Merle Robbins, who invented Uno in 1971, knew the significance of the number... but it's a cool fact!

It's a tradition to complete 108 salutations honoring the sun on the summer solstice, usually around June 21st. Kathy wrote the following short article when we led 108 Sun Salutations at the local Lululemon Store in Jacksonville. It was originally published in Natural Awakenings Magazine, a trademark of Natural Awakenings Publishing Company.

The Auspicious Number 108
by Kathy

The auspicious number of 108 refers to many things.

> The number of beads on a mala,
> the number of Hindu Gods,
> the number of sins in Tibet,
> the number of stitches on a baseball,
> and, most surprising, it's the emergency
> disaster number in India.

But today, it was to be the number of times I repeated the sacred salute to the sun to celebrate the Global Mala.

Nervousness, but mostly excitement and anticipation, filled me up as we began bringing the class to stillness. The yogic energy in the space sent a calming wave over me as we began the first set of 27. As I spoke of the dedication to inner peace, I watched my body flow through each movement, thankful for the strength and accepting of what was to come.

The second set of 27 was dedicated to family and friends. During the oh-so-familiar movements, gratefulness and abundance filled my soul as my life has been truly blessed with wonderful family and friends. So for these 27 salutations, my heart came alive.

Now halfway there, the short rest in Child's Pose was like water to a dying man in the desert. Back to Down Dog to start the third set for peace in the world. Not a small dedication by any means. And like the constant struggles around the globe, I felt my own small struggles with the repetitive poses but continued on without hesitation.

The final round was here at last and I knew I was home free. Just 27 more and, with a dedication to God, how could I falter? My finish was strong and rewarding, with an intense sense of accomplishment knowing that thousands of yogis around the world were feeling the same joy, bliss, and renewed dedication to peace on this most precious of days. The number 108 has left an impression on me both mentally and physically.

MANTRA JAPA PRACTICE

We love *365 Tao: Daily Meditations* by Deng Ming-Dao (Deng, 1992). The verse for day 226, paraphrased, is entitled *Repetition*:

> *"My prayer beads are strung upon my life span.*
> *I am not allowed to skip a single bead.*
> *Sometimes the bead is a seed. Or a bone, or crystal,*
> *or pure light. No matter what the next bead is,*
> *I must count it. Perform my daily austerities.*
> *Repeat. Repeat. Repeat. Until repetition becomes endurance."*

That really captures the meaning and power of repetition. The mala becomes a metaphor of our journey through life as we take each step, count each mala bead. Mantra Japa harnesses the power of the spoken word as an affirmation which is repeated so as to create new neural pathways for improving our habits.

Here are the ingredients for bringing this practice into your everyday life:

- Make a commitment and prioritize the practice into your day, or integrate it into your other practices, e.g., a personal yoga practice.
- Choose a mantra that truly has meaning to you on a very deep and personal level (some of our favorites are listed in Appendix 1).
- Know the meaning, but always chant the mantra in its original language. There are several online sources where you can find meanings, such as yogajournal.com and spiritvoyage.com.
- Set an intention based upon the meaning of the selected mantra.
- Choose how you wish to hold, or set up, space and time. Creating a meditative space is important, as you want an environment that supports you, that feels safe and comfortable. Perhaps you light some incense or choose a private part of your home. Either set a timer with a soothing alarm sound or use mala beads to keep count.
- Then, begin. You can repeat the mantra silently, whisper it, or sing. All forms of mantra repetition are powerful.

The power of mantras is found through mindful and intentional repetition. Over time, mantras become a part of you. They will reveal themselves as soft whispers at just the right time during the rest of your day. As you rewire the neural pathways of your brain, you will see the world in a different and more connected way.

IMPROVISATIONAL LIVING

During the final days of our yoga teacher training back in 2005, we were exposed to dynamic meditation, which is a form of meditation that includes spontaneous, unstructured movement. The purpose of this type of meditation is to take you out of your head, release any inhibitions, and let go. Our introduction was via a sixty-minute version in which most of the time was spent in improvisational movement to both meditative and up-tempo music. We were blindfolded to remove the vision sense so that we would not be distracted by others in terms of comparison or concerns, self-consciousness or shyness. There were no cameras or cell phones allowed, removing the temptation of selfies or group photos. This was intended to be an inward, deep practice of self-connection, self-expression, with no concern of the world around us. A couple of teacher moderators watched over about twenty-five of us so that we would feel safe from injury and bumping into others.

Honestly, it was one of the most amazing experiences we had in any of our trainings up to that point. The vibes of the music merged with the tissues of our bodies and spaciousness of our minds, resulting in a free-flowing, soulful expression of self. During the practice, the music progressed in tempo and intensity to a crescendo, then tempered down to gentle and meditative instrumentals, leading us into a long, deep Savasana. We simply dropped onto the floor wherever we were when directed to. It was like no other Savasana that we can recall.

We were so touched by this experience that we continued to seek out other versions of dynamic meditations or soulful movement. We now incorporate it into our longer meditation workshops and weekend immersion programs, and it has become a favorite among our students.

The improvisational aspect of this experience was key. Improvisation is a healthy dimension of expression. It relies upon the present moment; therefore, thoughts of past or future dissipate as we improvise. Some of us, present company included, spend much of our day in our left brain as we go through our routines of tasks, activities, jobs, and responsibilities. But we can shift into our right brain via improvisation. We need to get out of our minds, in a way.

There are several ways to bring improvisation into your life. Of course there is spontaneous or expressive movement in the form of dance or yoga, as mentioned above. Many painters and sculptors bring improvisation in quite well, just by seeing where the paint or clay takes them. If you like to write, do a spontaneous writing session with just a sheet of paper on which you spill your thoughts on the page with no regard to subject, sentence structure, punctuation, or grammar. If you are a musician, drop the sheet music or tablature and play a note, then another, or a chord. Let yourself play with no preconceived notion of tempo or melody. See where the music leads you. You will surprise yourself.

There are so many outlets for improvisation. Look to your life to find one that's right for you.

> *Kathy*: I never thought of myself as a very creative person, but yoga brought out in me a desire to spend more time cooking. If you think about it, cooking is the only art form that touches all five senses—sound, touch, taste, smell, and sight. Because we have been strict veg-

ans since 2006, I obviously had to spend a lot of time in the kitchen making meals for us since the selection of vegan restaurant options where we live is extremely limiting. I decided that I would try three to five new recipes a week, and fell in love with experimenting with different foods. Now, I feel like I might have a slight addiction, as I am constantly thinking of different things to cook and new recipes to try! In fact, I had the distinct pleasure of recipe testing for a cookbook that came out in 2017 called *Vegan Richa's Everyday Kitchen Cookbook*. I spent over a year helping her with recipes. I loved every minute of it—and, of course, Dennis really enjoyed eating it all as well!

These simple, unrestricted practices take us out of the left brain and bring us to the present moment. They are great stress relievers, as well.

SEEING AND LIVING
WITH REVERENCE

What if our religion was each other?
If our practice was our life?
If prayer was our words?
What if the Temple was the Earth?
If forests were our church?
If holy water—the rivers, lakes and oceans?
What if meditation was our relationships?
If the Teacher was life?
If wisdom was self-knowledge?
If love was the center of our being.

by Ganga White, ©1998 Ganga White,
All Rights Reserved, White Lotus Foundation,
whitelotus.org. *Reprinted with permission.*

These touching words remind us that we are part of the universe as a whole, that we are on a journey of learning, and that we are here in love.

As our integration of yoga progressed, we could not help but notice that our engagement with awareness and reverence became more consistent. We would take time to notice everything, from thoughts and feelings to what we said, how we spoke, how the five senses fed our perceptions. We would notice the simple things, like the sound of breezes through the oaks that form the canopy of our home, small lizards that like to sit in the warmth of the sun near our koi pond, the smell of the ocean as we walk on the sandy beach nearby. Everything became clearer and more alive with simple awareness.

Seeing and living with reverence means living with full acknowledgment of how precious life is, how delicate our ecological balance is, and how perfect we are.

A PRACTICE ACKNOWLEDGING
THE BEAUTY THAT SURROUNDS US

While on retreat at Rancho La Puerta in Mexico in 2017, we had the pleasure of meeting Phyllis Pilgrim. What an amazing and beautiful soul she is! Phyllis has been teaching yoga, meditation, Tai Chi, and Qi Gong at "The Ranch" since the early '80s. Among the key takeaways for us was this daily practice of hers, which she learned as a young child from her mother: Each day, see something beautiful, hear something beautiful, and say something beautiful. Do these three things each day to acknowledge and engage beauty.

We love this practice, as it reminds us to take notice of the beauty that surrounds us and how we can express beauty with our words. In doing so, you will enrich your life. The more we see and live with reverence, the more we become part of a positive shift and can create meaningful change for the betterment of others.

REFLECTIONS

"Reflection" means casting back a light,
mirroring, giving back, or showing an image.

Reflection, as though looking in a mirror, also represents our own reflected learning via assimilation, introspection, and contemplation. It seems the perfect term to represent key learnings from our personal practices, trainings, and studies. This section offers the culmination of knowledge and wisdom we have gained over the years. As we see it, these Reflections ponder how we can learn and benefit from these time-tested teachings. It is through these reflections that we found how yoga truly flourishes and where our true selves reside.

We share these reflections as authentically as we can express them. Each is written as a stand-alone, such that you do not have to read them sequentially and can come back to them individually. It is our hope that these might in some way touch you as they touched us and provide you with happiness and wellness as well as the means to simply "be."

THE JOURNEY BEGINS

Every journey starts at the beginning. Our beginning starts as we are, wherever we are. Complexity and sophistication are not required. In fact, intellect can get in the way; it's best to take on the qualities of a beginner for these practices.

Here is the thing. And it's a big one. The journey is not easy. That is, assuming you are even a seeker. Not everyone wants to go there.

Taking the yoga practice beyond a workout and into a deeper experience as a seeker is a spiritual endeavor. It's a journey on a path with pot holes, speed bumps, hills, and turns as you navigate the terrain of your life. It's not easy in the sense of learning about ourselves through the lens of the yoga sutras, but there's no rush on when it happens.

How we relate to our thoughts, feelings, and emotions, and how we perceive the world around us, is all up to us. Everything matters!

THE QUESTION BECAME "WHY?"

So why did we even bother with the pursuit of enlightenment, nirvana, or bliss? Why did we bother to practice yoga at all? It was an interesting thought for us. Couldn't we just have simply adjusted our lifestyle to a more harmonic path from our fast-paced, driven, and intense existences, without the need for yoga?

The issue with this line of thinking is that it presupposed that we were aware enough to recognize there was even an issue! It assumes that we were in touch with our true essences. It assumed knowledge and perspective that clearly were not present. Notice several key words in the previous three sentences: thinking, aware, knowledge, true essence, perspective, and present. Each of these words, when applied to our state of consciousness in our pre-yogic history, were dramatically different from their application today where we are deep into our yogic lifestyle.

You see, back then we did not see. We do not know what we do not know! Our vision back then was clouded and limited within our then-state of consciousness.

Dennis: I am reminded of a meeting we had with my cousin Lori Tapp back in 2002, in Asheville, North Carolina. It was a time during which Kathy and I were just starting to probe into our lives and just beginning to turn up the intensity of our yoga studies. Back then, Lori was a large animal vet specializing in holistic and alternative medicine. With a double Ph.D., she was extremely well-trained and an expert in her field. What many did not know was that she was a practitioner of Qi Gong and a meditator.

On this occasion I was complaining about my corporate job and how I could not change it or get out of it. I will never forget Lori listening with both attention and compassion as I went on and on. Then she replied, "You are stuck in your current consciousness!" In the moment, Kathy and I looked at one another and were uncertain what she really meant. She went on to explain that I was caught up within my current state of mind and experience and that I needed to break away or step back to see the experience from a different perspective.

You see, I was lost in the forest and could not see the trees. I was making assumptions about our situation. I had not learned about the Yamas and Niyamas and, frankly, was so caught up in my own ego. I was an amazing storyteller—actually, I'm not alone in this as we all are—and could justify anything to myself.

"You are caught in your current consciousness" was burned into the grey matter of my brain like a boldly printed tattoo. But it would take several years for us to fully grasp Lori's insight and to finally manifest our transformation.

Sadly, in November 2017, Lori lost her battle with cancer. She is acknowledged in the dedication of this book as she touched our lives with her insight and her light.

Through practice, as the touch of yoga worked its magic and as our new views of the world emerged, we realized that yoga is everywhere. It's written in the Upanishads that we are at one with all that's around us. As we look out into the world, we see us in the world and the world in us. We are all interconnected and interdependent. It's all about relationships—a simple concept, but it took years for us to realize.

As we start to notice and observe ourselves with even a partially open mind, we begin to consider and reflect upon our status, position, impact on, and connection to the world around us. Every part of ourselves and our existence is in relationship.

It all starts with you, yourself.

THE MAT AS A MIRROR

The title of this whole section, *Reflections*, also refers metaphorically to the mat itself. During the early years of our yoga practice and studies, we realized our mats were integral to our experience. We developed a love of them much like a favorite pair of blue jeans. They were just as important as the rest of our apparel, props, or accessories.

Throughout your practice, the yoga mat takes on the qualities of a mirror and thus reflects the state of your being during practice. Each pose and transition is an energetic representation of us at that particular moment of practice. Whether or not you are aware of the moment or even fully present, the mat supports the practice and the body and is your connection to earth through gravity.

Not to get too nerdy, and certainly this is not rocket science, but the mat also provides a protective barrier of support on which to practice as well as defines a safe region within which we practice. Today, there are so many mats to choose from—different sizes, designs, and materials, not to mention price points. Yes, even something as basic as a yoga mat has evolved with commercialization in the western world.

No matter the details of design or price, the mat length and width define a territory or boundary of separation from others in open yoga classes. In addition, your height, including your fullest reach above your head, establishes the third dimension of space on a mat, thereby making an imaginary cube. Within this three-dimensional space is a safe place in which to practice "privately," even in a highly populated group yoga class. It's here where we experience and express ourselves through the yoga practice.

In terms of support, the mat provides traction and cushioning properties to facilitate safe transitions and stabilize long-held poses. Interestingly, we also noticed that our mats showed wear from our movements. As we practice, we create scuffs and pits, wear and tear that accumulate over time. This wear is unique to each yoga practitioner and is also a signature.

When we compared them, our mats were very different, although we were practicing together and doing the same classes and sequences. In some ways they were like impressionistic art. These impressions of our yoga practices were recorded as our individual wear patterns.

As former long-distance runners, we began to look at these wear patterns as we did our running shoes. Wear patterns in running shoes are indicative of healthy, efficient technique...or otherwise. You can look at your mat the same way. What is the wear pattern telling you? It takes a while and a lot of time on the mat to really get this and see what we are talking about, so don't worry if this doesn't come naturally at first.

The mat is also a metaphor of our lives. Wherever you go, there you are! Remember? Again, that quote always works as a reminder. When we show up on our mats, we show up as we are at that very moment. Not as we were yesterday and certainly not as we hope to be tomorrow. We are alive NOW. In this very present moment.

Our bodies are our most tangible present moment asset, as they live only in the present. It's only in our minds that we "time travel" as we live in the past or future. Most of the time, we are stuck with worries of past or anxiety of the future, and these thoughts distract us from the most obvious aspect of life: the present moment. The mat can become a reminder of this very fact. As we step on our mat, we are entering the spaciousness of presence. If we reel in our awareness to this reality, using our mat as a tool and a foundation, then we can reap the rewards of our practice.

> *Kathy*: The yoga mat is one of the few places where you can lose yourself and find yourself at the same time. I love when I am taking someone else's class and I have that yoga moment where I completely forget where I am and what I am doing. I am lost in the present moment. And there are other times when I have an "aha" moment during a pose and notice a particular pattern or habit. From one of my early experiences, I remember we were in a Yin Yoga class and we were holding a floor-based posture for five minutes, and all I could think about was how much I wanted to get out of that pose. It seemed to be pure torture at the time. My "aha" moment was when I realized that my usual pattern is to run when things get tough, and that's exactly what I was trying to do in that Yin pose! I sat with that revelation and studied my behavior, then laughed at myself because, at that moment, I think my eyes were open to another dimension of the yoga practice and I loved it even more!

The yoga mat is a mirror of our energetic state and captures impressions representing the nature and duration of our practice. The key, however, is to honestly observe, notice, and listen from within—and then *be willing to shift,* be willing to change, and be willing to be guided by your inner truth.

Do not take your mat for granted. Treat it as a sacred and integral part of your yoga. At first, this may not make sense. But later, as your practice progresses, you will find that your mat might become like an oasis or safe refuge. The mat becomes more than just a piece of rubber, vinyl, or plastic that you throw on the floor. It's your own private place to get rid of any excess mental or emotional baggage. With this kind of power, it should be treated with care and respect. We see people bringing in their dirty, sandy, folded-up mats to class and think, "Is that how they treat all their prized possessions?" Also, try not to step on anyone else's yoga mat for hygiene reasons and also because, hopefully, they think of their mat as a sacred place just like you!

So, if you do not have your own yoga mat, buy one!

CONNECTING THE DOTS

During his graduation commencement address at Stanford University in 2005, Steve Jobs spoke of connecting the dots of your past, with "dots" meaning major events or milestones in your life history. His point was that you can only connect the dots in your past, not your future. Whether by faith or karma, we hope the dots of the past will lead to and guide us toward a positive future.

We came to this relationship each having our own collection of dots from our prior lives. How amazing—and, let's say, divinely guided—that we should meet up and merge, having come from such different places and upbringings.

It reminds us of how spiritual teacher Michael Singer speaks of all the forces of the universe coming together to create each moment of our lives (Mickey's Talk Nights, Temple of the Universe, 2016). Yoga master Sri Dharma Mitra notes that enlightenment is when you realize that each moment was, in fact, perfect as it was and as it should have been (Interview in Wanderlust magazine, 2017). Within this context, it is truly awesome and humbling to be part of such a flow.

When we stepped into our first yoga class, we had no idea that this would become another of these major dots in our lives, a dot that adjusted the direction and purpose of our life journey together. It was monumental.

Dennis: Steve Jobs' speech was very inspirational to me. We are so thankful that he gave this particular talk, and that it was recorded for all to benefit. His reminders about the dots of the past and finding direction for your future further motivated our transformation. I look back on my life to this point and see so many dots:

- As a teenager, I was very interested in martial arts, which gave me a little bit of understanding and appreciation for Eastern philosophies. This would tie in later as we delved into the yoga traditions.

- In college, I had to take many oral exams which gave me, the introverted kid, the confidence to speak in front of people and engage the audience. This comes in very handy teaching yoga classes and workshops!

- Against my parents' wishes, I turned down several really good job offers after receiving my undergrad degree so that I could pursue a Master's. Weirdly enough, I chose to do my thesis on sound transmission, which helps me to understand and explain the science of crystal bowls as a healing modality to our yoga students.

- Staying in school that extra time for grad school made it possible for the position in Toledo to open up, where I met Kathy.

- Taking several creative writing classes together opened up another outlet for expression off the yoga mat, leading us to write this book.

Kathy: I find a similar pattern with my own dots:

- My grandmother always told me, "You can do anything you set your mind to," which I believed from an early age. This taught me to never be afraid of change and step out on faith.

- I decided to try out for cheerleading the summer of 1970, even though I was a thirteen-year-old chubby kid with glasses and not part of the "cool kids" club. I lost a bunch of weight that summer, got contacts, and by the fall tryouts I had confidence and made the squad. I went on to become co-captain and cheered for six years. This built a fearless ability to be in front of crowds and be myself, which is crucial for a yoga teacher.

- I accepted a promotion in Toledo against my strong southern family's urging that it was way too cold "up there" and "Who would want to live in Toledo, anyway?" But it put me in perfect position to meet up with Dennis six months later.

- At one of my jobs, I was asked to write and create technical brochures for a product line, even though that was not in my job description. I took to it like a duck to water and really enjoyed the creative process. Now I create flyers for our yoga retreats, workshops, and events.

Could each of these major dots in our lives be a convergence of energies, like vortices, which manifest in a single event which is in fact monumental? We believe so! Energies can be magnified when combined. Look to nature, where we see the power of the wind combine with the flow of a river to create large waves. Look to science and consider the Doppler effect, in which sound from a moving train is louder to observers standing ahead of the train because the speed of the train amplifies the original sound, but is lower to observers standing behind as the train moves away at high speed. (Any surprise that we use an example from sound and vibration? Probably not!)

> *Kathy*: I'm going to spill some of Dennis' beans here by telling you that he was a straight A student in grad school. He studied all the time and took it very seriously. But me, not so much. I heard a statement early on in my high school years that the A students end up working for the B and C students because the A students are more focused on their studies and are not as well-rounded as the B and C students. The B and C students spend more time building relationships (e.g., partying or other social outlets), while the A students don't know how to work well with others when they get out in the real world, away from academia. So I was perfectly happy to make Bs and Cs. At Clemson, I didn't really choose my major; it kind of chose me. We had to declare a major before our first semester, which is nuts if you think about. What eighteen-year-old has a clue about what they want to be?

> I started out in pre-veterinary medicine because I loved animals. But science was the hardest thing for me to grasp, so I went to a counselor and asked what I could major in that did not require any science. They suggested accounting, and I thought, well, I'm good with numbers, so that should be okay.

The next semester, I took my first accounting class and found that all those debits and credit columns were confusing, so back to the Admin building I went to find out what I could major in with no science and no accounting! The nice lady recommended business administration, so the first semester of my sophomore year, I took a marketing class and fell in love with all the business courses. Little did I know that this business degree would really come in handy when I was forty-six and marketing a yoga business! This was definitely one of those dots that Steve Jobs referenced in his speech!

The dots of our past led us here. Now, as a couple, we co-create the dots of our lives while realizing that everything matters. Perhaps you cannot connect dots into your future, but you *can* extrapolate and create a trajectory defined by intention and purpose.

IS BEING PRESENT ENOUGH?

Today we find so many references to the present moment. For us, it's comforting to know that awareness of the present moment is rising and mindfulness has become a household word. Living life with mindful awareness and presence releases us from attachments and aversions, in turn softening our egocentric dominance and resulting in a more relaxed, harmonious lifestyle. Certainly the world would be a much better place if more of us lived our lives mindfully. But what if we could squeeze just a bit more out of the present moment?

Quantum physics and several leading authors on the subject of relativity, epigenetics, and the placebo effect note that all possibilities lie in the present moment. In other words, when we are truly present in the moment, we are able to shape our experiences.

Consider a person who is anxious most of the time. This is an individual who is likely very concerned about the future, perhaps a "controller" personality type. So much energy and emphasis is placed on these worries that this individual misses present-moment opportunities to redirect or influence his or her outcome in a more positive way. To be so future-thought driven is to miss the short-term view, to miss the forest for the trees.

Similarly, someone who is worried about the past is obsessed about not letting go. Perhaps letting go is one of our biggest challenges in life. We are so attached to our past, our possessions, and our identities. As with the anxious person, the worrisome person misses present-moment opportunities since their mental view, their mind's eye, is toward the past and so misses what's directly in their present.

Each of these individuals are examples of how many of us live: caught with excessive thoughts, stuck in the past or future. Both are negative views and will result in dis-ease over time. Present-moment awareness helps loosen the grasp of these attachments.

What if we take this one step further? Can we not only realize and engage the possibilities of the present moment for ourselves, but also uplift the present moment for the benefit of others? In so doing, we have made a positive contribution from presence which will reflect a positive result or reaction back to us!

This sounds like the well-known Law of Attraction and Law of Cause and Effect. Yes, indeed! As energetic beings, we are in a constant state of change or flux. We are dynamic, multi-dimensional, energetic beings involved in continual energy transformation and exchanges with the world around us. For the worrisome pessimist, positive present-moment awareness and choices will soften the anchor of past burdens. For the anxious Type A controller (as Dennis was), present-moment awareness with positive choices will soften rough edges.

We each have an opportunity to shape our life experiences with mindful awareness, therefore uplifting the present moment.

ALIGNMENT: SENSING FROM THE INSIDE OUT

In todays' world of yoga, there is a great deal of emphasis on alignment, primarily anatomical alignment. We have found through our own practice, studies, and teaching that a little goes a long way. A little is essential, but over-emphasized can create another form of concern or stress.

Perhaps we can learn from the Tao. Consider this, from Day 212, "Form," in Deng Ming-Dao's book, *365 Tao: Meditations* (Ming-Dao, 1992):

> *At first, form is needed.*
> *The doubt and inhibition must be dispelled.*
> *Eventually, form is celebrated with joy,*
> *And expression becomes formless.*

As he discusses in this verse, using a dancer as an example, the novice student must drill constantly on the basics. Emphasis is placed upon each step, movement, and structure. All must become natural. Once it does, then the dance becomes an expression of joy and spontaneity. Form then emerges with grace, originality, and beauty.

Form in the context of the yoga asana practice is alignment. Although basic alignment is necessary to develop a pose and to fully experience and express it during practice, it seems some teachers and styles place so much emphasis on anatomical alignment that they miss the point of the practice. Certainly this is all with good intentions. However, this focus seems highly influenced by the fitness industry and, to a lesser extent, has a touch of ego behind it. In addition, deep physiological and anatomical detail really are subjects for deeper discussions, such as in workshops and teacher training modules, rather than in the limits of a short ninety-minute group class.

Here in the US, the most popular forms of yoga fall under the power vin-yasa flow umbrella. These dynamic and externally-motivated forms look and feel like calisthenics. Yoga has evolved and will continue to do so, but the direction of yoga today emphasizes the physical with less focus on the mind-body-spirit system as a whole. Relative to ego, it seems we love to make things more complicated than they really need to be. Have we implied that before? Well, it's worth repeating!

> *Kathy*: Of course this is true in other aspects of our lives. Alignment can become a means of spewing knowledge to feed our ego. We have seen many teachers pontificate endlessly throughout an entire class with alignment cues alone. During our teacher training, I remember vividly Stephanie Keach telling us that anyone can learn the postures and call the poses, but a great yoga teacher is one who can add richness to the commentary and not just talk about alignment–a teacher who can bring in various elements of the ancient texts, share the Yoga Sutras, and discuss the deeper dimensions of yoga. This richness is what students will return to again and again. Someone who simply focuses on the physical part of the class and does nothing but instruct by talking about the poses is, to us, simply a fitness instructor!

Whoa! There, I said it! I hope I didn't offend any of you, but that's how we view it. In our world, we feel that if we only speak about the poses, then we are doing our students a huge disservice, falling short as teachers, and understating what yoga is really about.

An article written by Jenni Rawlings (Yoga International, 4/13/2017) regarding the "Top 5 Movement Science Insights for Teachers" captures several really key points. In it, she reminds us that alignment is mostly about load optimization. If we were lifting heavy weights, then certainly more emphasis on physical alignment is necessary. But this is yoga. Our body is our weight and, as we shift in and out of poses and transitions with mindful awareness and the guidance of the nervous system, we will adjust and re-align so as to avoid injury. Our bodies are miraculous, with their innate intelligence! We should give ourselves and our students more credit.

In the above paragraph, the key phrase is *mindful awareness*. To practice yoga safely, we must be in a state of active listening from the inside out: listening to our senses and sensations; listening to our tissues and our breath; listening to our feelings and emotions. Active listening guides our bodies into proper alignment. This level of mindful awareness takes time to develop.

Remember, as we noted in the section on the 5 E's, those new to the practice of yoga need to place a lot of emphasis on alignment and technique. Beginner workshops and private sessions are perfect for this. A large yoga class is not the right place for this kind of detailed guidance; although it may be good for new students, it can sometimes frustrate the experienced student. A teacher needs proper training in physical alignment but also should queue the poses to match the audience, all while watching the students with a highly trained eye looking for gross errors.

In our view, alignment is a holistic concept. It should account for all aspects of our being—our mental, emotional, and energetic selves as well as our physical. Be grateful for the autonomic nervous system and listen to its messages. As our practice advances, awareness and focus on alignment shifts from the physical and anatomical to the energetic. This shift in awareness lets us connect with the deeper levels of our energy, meridians, and chakras, and tap into our inner essence.

TRANSITIONS

"We are all verbs, not nouns."
— *Deepak Chopra*

Life is in constant change. Everything is moving and in a state of flux. Some things, like inanimate objects, appear on the surface as not moving, but on an atomic level, they are vibrating, just like we are! So really, nothing is truly stationary.

How we move through life, how we position ourselves with our attitudes and awareness, all matters. The how and why—the method and intention of our movements that lead to a destination, position, or posture—matter.

As Mozart said, "Music is not the notes, but the silence in between." The transitions of our lives and the transitions between yoga postures during practice are like the silence between the notes of music.

> *Dennis*: As I mentioned, I used to travel to Washington, DC on business frequently. Back then I was working with lobbyists and government agencies, posturing and positioning for procurements as a defense contractor. It was intense and high pressure, to say the least. Once I found yoga, I would go to a yoga studio in Georgetown

in the evenings. It was an intense, hot power flow class, Baptiste Power Vinyasa to be specific, and I loved it.

One evening I attended a large class in which we were moving through a series of warrior poses. During a transition into Warrior II, I made a strong, fast, aggressive entry with a very intense expression, which caught the teacher's eye. She came over and asked that I chill out a little and soften into and out of the poses, rather than force my way as though it were a full-contact karate match.

Yes, that was a wake-up call for me. I had brought my aggressive and competitive self onto the mat and into my practice. I was not tapping into the equanimity that lies between effort and ease; I was missing the whole point of the practice. That lesson stuck with me. Even today, when I feel my transitions into postures even *start* to resemble that old Type A personality that I was back then, I remember to soften and ease into the shape and then seek an optimum expression of energy.

Transitions on the mat and off the mat are the same. Place the same care and mindfulness upon the transitions in life that you do within the poses of a yoga practice.

HOLISTIC HEALTH AND HEALING

A Google search of holistic health generates over nine million hits! Wow, this is a huge subject.

"Holistic healing" is the view that health involves the body, mind, and spirit together. They are intimately and directly linked. It's like a three-legged stool; if one leg is broken, the stool is at risk of collapse.

Over the years, this became more obvious to us. Although we are not medical practitioners or professionals, we deal with healing and prevention on a regular basis as yoga teachers.

We view yoga as a holistic healing modality. The medical benefits of yoga and meditation have been well documented in peer-reviewed studies by scientists and the medical community. All you need is to practice. Practice, practice, practice.

Our views of health and wellness have evolved over the years, especially since finding yoga. Previously, in our pre-yoga lives, we simply followed what the doctor ordered, without question. Sounds appropriate and straightforward—but, as we learned later, it was a cursory view and somewhat distorted.

Dennis: As I mentioned before, I had my health issues and bottomed out with prescriptions and my ever-growing heftiness. It was interesting: As I look back on the early months of my practice, yoga postures really were instrumental in my taking ownership of my own health. There's nothing like arm balances like crow (Balasana) or eight-limbed (Astavakrasana) to build awareness of your girth! Twisted postures, too, place such emphasis on core energy and the geometry of the midline that to progress in yoga, you will naturally want to manage your weight.

Also, keeping a uniform breath, or constant pranayama method, during practice really tops off this awareness. To simply practice Surya Namaskar A, the simplest version, with the right breath control can be enough to make a measurable and sustainable difference in weight loss as well as overall well-being. In my case, it was instrumental in shifting my health.

Again, yoga is about relationships. In the case of health, it's personal; it's about you with yourself. Yes, our health impacts those around us, especially family members, but to observe, notice, assess, and make changes—well, that's up to us and us alone. Yoga has a way of opening our eyes, allowing us to see. It empowers us to inquire, to question, to not take for granted or make assumptions. Through yoga we seek truth.

Any discussion of health and wellness runs directly into the issue of Western versus Eastern medicine, allopathic versus alternative or integrative medicine. Our view is that all have their place. We have had our share of both with great results. In recent years, many leading medical institutions have been integrating alternative therapies such as acupuncture, healing touch, meditation, mindfulness, and plant-based nutrition. We are pleased to see more and more openness to the so-called New Age methods—which are really old age or original, as they predated much of the relatively young allopathic methods.

As yoga teachers, we cannot diagnose or provide treatment. However, when practicing or teaching yoga, we are certainly walking on the edge of issues associated with health, happiness, and dis-ease. By its very nature, yoga is a holistic healing modality with many therapeutic elements. Here is what we mean:

Healing = (Right Energy + Mindful Awareness) x N

> *Kathy*: Did you think you could get through the book without an equation? Of course not! This is how Dennis' mind works!

Let's look at this more closely.

Right Energy = The right integrative therapy, treatment, or procedure appropriate for the ailment, trauma, or issue. This might be yoga, acupuncture, lymphatic massage, or anything else.

Mindful Awareness = The combined, positive focus of awareness, attention, steady breath method, attitude, and emotion on the part of the patient.

N = The number of repetitions or sessions with a particular treatment. Alternative therapies typically require more than one session. By their nature they work on the subtle energies of the body, and therefore require an accumulated effect over a period of time.

There are a few other things required to make this equation effective.

- The patient should be in a present-moment state of awareness and attention.
- Breathe in accordance with the appropriate treatment method. If no other form of pranayama is specified, use long, slow, deep breathing.
- The right positive attitude, e.g., cooperative and open attitude to receive treatment.
- Consciously choosing and willing to step forward with a modality, i.e., not being forced or coerced.
- Feel the emotion as though the treatment is already successful; literally believe and feel as you will feel in complete health.

Intention is the overarching key here. Your intention must be to be a positive participant and a catalyst of your own healing via the modality of choice. Seeing and believing in the positive outcome even before treatment begins and throughout the treatment process is also key.

As mentioned above, Dennis had been prescribed meds years ago, just after we found yoga. We both sensed this was an over-reaction by the doctor and we felt somewhat misguided. It seemed like a classic example of throwing medications at symptoms with no in-depth analysis, Western medicine at its worst. The more we thought about it, the more we felt betrayed. We lost trust in our doctor. Dennis went into a mode of research on alternative methods to lower blood pressure naturally (recall the nerd tendency). We learned that taking a holistic view was key to a natural approach to health and wellness. The integration of diet, exercise, and stress reduction would be the right path.

To apply this to the equation: The right energy was the combined practices of yoga, meditation, and dietary change. Mindful awareness was a given. Right attitude was tied to willingness to do the work and to see the effect emotionally as though it had already happened, even during the process.

In addition, we looked at our lifestyle and made adjustments, leading to our change in careers to reduce stress. Over a thirty-day period, we took blood pressure readings twice per day and tracked the data to be sure improvements were real and stable. Dennis was able to naturally get off both medications and even stabilize his weight, which has been stable ever since.

BREATH AS A METRONOME

To practice yoga without breath awareness is not yoga. In the fourth limb of the eight limbs of yoga as presented in the Yoga Sutras, Pranayama presents breath awareness as integral to the practice. Breath awareness is essential and required for yoga practice. Other wisdom and contemplative ancient practices such as Buddhism, Tai Chi, and Qi Gong also place emphasis on how we manage, manipulate, and integrate the breath within the practice and our daily lives.

The ancient sages, rishis, and yogis learned through intuitive, empirical, and experiential means. They observed nature and noticed that the length of life for various animals appeared to be related to their rate of breath. Elephants had very slow rates of breath and lived long lives, whereas hummingbirds had very high rates of respiration and very short lives. Over time, some of these rishis and sages came to believe that to extend our breath—that is, to extend and optimize our use of prana— would extend our lives. While they did not have the science and technology then that we do today, modern Western medicine is looking more and more at the correlation between breath and well-being.

Our survival depends upon the right amounts and the right balance of food, sleep, water, and breath. Among these, breath is the one element which we cannot live without for the shortest amount of time. Each of us is different, but the averages indicate we die after three to four minutes without air, three to four days without water, and three to four months without food. Breath is basic to our lives.

THE EARTH BREATHES; WE BREATHE

Consider our connection to the earth as it relates to our breath. The very oxygen we breathe comes from the ocean and plants. And, in turn, plants inhale the carbon dioxide that we exhale. As air and breath are part of the life force, or prana, that sustains us, we are ultimately dependent upon nature. The earth's breath flows in the form of wind and weather; from the soft textures of a gentle summer breeze to the fierce, bone-chilling winds of a winter storm, we feel the earth breathe. Humankind can do whatever it chooses as a collective, as a species on the earth, but nature continues, never missing a beat, never worrying, never forcing, and ultimately it rules.

Our lives are connected to the earth's breath, part of an amazing eco-system that is in a delicate balance in the context of continued support of human life. We could segue right into a dissertation on global warming, pollution, and humanity's seeming lack of earth consciousness, but we will not. Perhaps in the next book.

Through our birth, we arrive with our first inhalation and we exit this world with a final exhalation. The breaths in between are up to us, and these breaths of our lives follow the tempo and texture of our consciousness in each passing moment. Our breath, our time as it passes, and our experiences all flow and change—as does nature. This is because we are part of nature and nature is a part of us; we breathe together with the earth and with nature. Together we are interconnected and interdependent for as long as we are here on earth.

THE INHALATION IS A RESUSCITATION

In November of 2017, we taught at the Sivananda Ashram in the Bahamas on "Food as Spiritual Path." Our sessions looked at this very important subject from a yogic perspective. One of our points was that air is food. The inhalation leads to assimilation of air as the air is transformed and converted via an oxygen exchange and then transmitted via the blood throughout our bodies and into every cell.

After one of our sessions, we had a conversation with a Swami in which he added his perspective regarding breath. He suggested that we might think about each inhale as a resuscitation from God, saving our life for the next breath. What a beautiful and meaningful view, that our breath is the ultimate gift of our lives, moment by moment, breath by breath.

Our autonomic nervous system keeps us alive on autopilot. It's so good that we do not have to think about breathing or giving the command consciously to inhale and exhale or tell our heart to beat. It's a miraculous system. However, because it's automatic, and by our nature, we take our breath for granted. We just let it happen. Setting aside the link of breath with our heart and mind, and considering that we could only live three to four minutes without air, it's somewhat of a paradox that we do not appreciate each breath more.

SUKHA OR DUKKHA

Yoga is empowering.

We learn that there is little in the world that we can control. However, the one thing we can control is our attitude. Our attitude is a key underlying element of our health, wellness, and happiness. Attitude is directly related to happiness. Remember the Law of Cause and Effect and the Law of Attraction? It's as Einstein said: You choose the energy you want.

A negative attitude is negative energy, which will attract negative energy. It will radiate into your world and touch those around you, shifting *their* energies. A negative attitude internally causes stress within, and the negative energy of reflection and attraction adds to that self-imposed stress. This is not a good exchange with the world and not a win-win for you or those around you.

Alternatively, a positive attitude has quite the opposite effect. A positive attitude is positive energy. Our posture in the world with a positive attitude is open and welcoming, warm and supportive. As such, we are received as positive energy and, in turn, our experiences are positive—or at least neutral.

Here is the amazing thing: Our attitude is up to us! Yes, our happiness is up to us and it is directly related to our attitude. It's our choice.

Sukha is the Sanskrit word for happiness. Dukkha is the word for suffering, the opposite of happiness. As they say, pain is inevitable as part of our worldly existence, but suffering is optional. This doesn't mean we can always choose what happens to us. The optional part is how we choose to experience life in general or specific challenging situations.

The choice between sukha and dukkha is up to us, each one of us! That's the empowering and exciting part—but it's also the challenging part, as it's all about our attitude.

YOGA IN DIFFICULT TIMES

"Every life experience, no matter how "tragic," contains a hidden lesson. When we discover and acknowledge the hidden gift that is there, a healing takes place."

— *David R. Hawkins,*
Letting Go: The Pathway of Surrender

Life happens, and it's not always rainbows and unicorns.

The Taoist or Daoist philosophy of ancient China, with roots dating back to the 4th century BCE, so eloquently presents the dualistic nature of life here on earth, our connection to nature, and the underlying, all-encompassing matrix which runs through everything. Taoism is about living in harmony with this all-encompassing matrix, known as the Tao. Yin and Yang characterize this duality, representing the opposing qualities or forces of nature. These dualities in the universe are co-existent, co-essential, and cycle within nature. You cannot have one without the other. To know happiness, you must know and experience sadness. As the sun rises in the east, it casts a shadow on the western face of the mountain. The shadow exists because of the sun. They are interconnected.

These extremes are co-essential in that they need each other in order for each to be known. Emotions, feelings, light, and life in general cycle, as does nature. Nature ebbs and flows as seasons change. Our lives ebb and flow as each moment passes. Difficult times are a part of life. Take loss or grief, for example. You can ignore it, suppress it, or self-medicate, but that only leads to prolonging the grieving process. As energetic beings, it's important to feel and express our emotions. Within such situations there lies a lesson or a nugget for our growth and development.

Look at it another way, and consider difficult times as a part of "Earth school." Our existence here, by its nature, will include times of sadness and challenge. Reflect upon the Hindu God Ganesha, who is the remover of obstacles—but will also *place* an obstacle in your path for a special lesson or purpose. Our issues and negative experiences, though, are not as much due to the obstacle or situation itself. Our issues and negative experiences are really due to our *relationship* with the obstacle or situation. However, shifting perspective and focusing on the relationship like this is easier said than done.

> *Dennis*: *Convergence* and *compression* are the two words that capture how I have felt in recent times of challenge, particularly in negative situations which lead to an inevitable end and with no alternatives. These are the most intense. During such times, it's as though there is as a narrowing or tunneling of negative experience in which the walls seem to be closing in. It's a convergence of awareness within the challenge or issue as it progresses, resulting in a heaviness, a feeling of compression as though the air is thicker, gravity stronger, and the weight of the world is upon me. This can manifest from any part of our life's experiences or from any source, career change, political upheaval, or financial turmoil. It's especially true for me in cases of terminal illness and loss of loved ones, which were the sources we

were dealing with during the last half of 2017.

It's in these times of convergence and compression that yoga and meditation become the internal support system. They provide a safe haven in which to turn inward, observe, and listen. It's during difficult times that we are tested. We are here to live life on all levels, the full range of experiences, feelings, and emotions. Within each challenge, there lies a message or lesson. Many times, I am reminded by my inner teacher that it's about my relationship with the situation, not the situation itself. In such circumstances, I am reminded of perhaps the most difficult lesson for us all, to let go. Yoga and meditation are the means to connect with the light and to listen in silence for the messages and lessons within.

You cannot be alive and avoid life. You cannot just stick your head in the sand or hit the escape button. We must be at peace with life, with ourselves as we are, and learn acceptance of the world as it is. Now, this is not to say we simply go passive. Actually, quite to the contrary; we learn to allow and deal with life in an empathetic and compassionate way.

YOGA IS YOUR BEST FRIEND

Times of trouble and difficulty are when we need support, and it is during these times when the relationship of yoga has a quality and supportive power like your best friend. We think of it this way: Yoga meets you where you are, unconditionally. No matter what is happening in your life, yoga is always there.

It's during these times when yoga practice is most important. To get on your mat and move mindfully with your breath, perhaps with no specific sequence or purpose in mind. To tap into the emotion or consider the situation as it is with straightforward observation. To be a witness of it and then listen for a lesson or message. Is it possible there is indeed a lesson from this situation which will lead to a better you?

It's in this context and under these situations, when it seems life is dealing you a bad hand, that the practice of yoga, meditation, and mindfulness really delivers.

TO GURU OR NOT TO GURU

According to the Buddha as recorded in the Kalama Sutra (Wikipedia):

Do not go upon what has been acquired by repeated hearing,
nor upon tradition,
nor upon rumor,
nor upon what is in a scripture,
nor upon surmise,
nor upon an axiom,
nor upon specious reasoning,
nor upon a bias towards a notion that has been pondered over,
nor upon another's seeming ability,
nor upon the consideration, The monk is our teacher,

Kalamas, when you yourselves know: "These things are good; these things are not blamable; these things are praised by the wise; undertaken and observed, these things lead to benefit and happiness," enter on and abide in them.

This teaching by the Buddha has been shared and paraphrased by many over the centuries since it was first taught and later recorded. As we consider this teaching and apply it in our own lives and practices, it's all about not accepting anything as truth, from any source, until we assess it for ourselves in our own lives and relative to our ethics, morals, and values. In addition, we then determine if the subject or information is for the betterment of all beings—all *sentient* beings, not just human beings. And if it is for the betterment of all, then do that, believe that, think that, learn that.

To guru or not to guru is a compelling issue. Do you need a guru in order to practice yoga or pursue the deeper dimensions of the yoga practice? A guru is a spiritual teacher who sheds light upon darkness. They impart knowledge and wisdom on fundamental issues of life and, in some traditions, initiate disciples. The word *guru* literally means to go from darkness (Gu) to light (Ru).

"Guru" as a concept can bring up many visions and create concerns relative to Western thinking, religion, and individual moral and ethical values. The word itself can conjure up misconceptions of what it's really about. Yoga, as with any organized effort, group, belief system, or even religion, can fall victim to the egos of humans and their transgressions.

To find, follow, and devote yourself to a guru is one path in the journey of yoga. However, in our opinion, it's not the only path.

In the ancient days of past, the need for a guru might have made more sense. Those were the days of teaching mostly via vocal transmission, teacher to student, or in small groups. This was long before the advent of technology as we know it. It's important to remember that ancient teachings, or any history for that matter, must be taken in the context of its time. These are not those days, and the world is so much different now—and only *different*, not necessarily better or worse.

Our view is from the perspective of contemporary Western yogis. Our training has been exclusively in the US. It's all we know. We are simply noting that in our experience of yoga, a guru is not necessary to be a serious student, practitioner, and teacher of yoga. Certainly, a guru is not needed to integrate yoga across your lifestyle as a means for self-improvement.

We do, however, believe that having a good teacher—or several—is very important for our learning and development. A teacher who is authentic, who walks the talk, lives it, and breathes it is what defines a good teacher, in our opinion. We are not fans of a guru or teacher who would require an unfiltered devotion and dedication.

Our opinions regarding the need for a guru are molded by the various historic and ancient texts of yoga. The Yoga Sutras are always an anchor for us. In the Niyamas, we find Ishvara Pranidhana, which presents the idea of surrender as we are part of something much larger, we are part of the universe, spirit, or perhaps even your God. Each of us is part of a whole, which is the vast, infinite, universal Self and is our ultimate Teacher. This is our interpretation and how we apply this Niyama in our lives.

A parallel philosophical and historic reference comes from the ancient Buddhist chant, *Om Mani Padme Om*, or *The Jewel Lies within the Lotus*. As a metaphor, the jewel reflects light and the lotus represents the flower of the heart. The chant itself is a chant of purification on multiple levels and for multiple afflictions. It's the combination of our toxicity—mentally, emotionally, and energetically—and the afflictions of our lives that dim the outer layers such that we miss our inner essence, beauty, and truth.

> *"I have been a seeker and I still am,*
> *but I stopped asking the books and the stars.*
> *I started listening to the teaching of my Soul."*
>
> — *Rumi*

No one else lives your life. Yes, there are great teachers and masters of many disciplines and traditions. There are gifted spiritual leaders throughout the world. We are all here today standing upon the shoulders of the saints, sages, rishis, masters, and forest dwellers of the past. But, ultimately, we are responsible for our lives, our choices, and our actions.

> *Dennis*: Often during our home practices, and sometimes for our open public classes, we light a candle which is placed front and center between us. We do this as a symbol of the light of the guru within us. The flame of our inner teacher speaks and guides us via intuitive communications and inner sensations. The candle reminds us of the sacred connection and unlimited, everlasting, ever-present light. The ultimate guru lies within each of us.

THE PARADOX OF PERFECTION

One of Kathy's favorite quotes is:

"Perfection is the highest form of self-abuse."
— Anne Wilson Schaef (variation)

As yogis, we tether our practice and lifestyle to the Yoga Sutras. Self-abuse relates directly to Ahimsa, while observation of self, Svadhyaya, is the key to realization and growth.

> *Kathy*: Growing up, perfection was expected. In our appearance, cleanliness, how we kept our bedrooms, penmanship, everything. I remember once when I was a kid and I was coloring in my coloring book, I was not allowed to color outside the lines. And the faces had to be colored what we thought of then as flesh color, the sky blue, etc. It really stifled my creativity and I grew up thinking I was not a very creative person. However, yoga was able to help me overcome some of my perfectionism tendencies and bring my creative side back to the surface.

Perfection is defined as a state of being complete, flawless, and faultless. Throughout our lives, many of us—dare we say most of us—are conditioned to seek perfection. We are guided or molded by our upbringing, culture, education, experiences, activities, and professions. Culture includes social media, advertising, promotion, and commercialism. We learn to compare, judge, and be dissatisfied. We lack contentment and become driven and even competitive as we strive to be better, acquire more, and achieve.

We are not saying goals, acquisition, and achievement are bad per se. The issue is our relationship with them. In the context of perfection, the underlying issues are comparison, judgement, and fear.

THE PRESSURE OF PERFECTION

To be complete, flawless, and faultless—the very definition of perfect— are huge expectations of ourselves. Talk about pressure! How can you live in this world and truly be flawless and faultless? Who do you know who is either of these, let alone both?

Flaws and faults have both physical and emotional qualities. As for the emotional, isn't this where mercy and forgiveness come into play? We all have our shortcomings or faults. We must forgive ourselves and others.

As for the physical aspect, we all have faults. Even the models who are used in fashion photography are not flawless. Digital photographic alterations, filters, and touch-ups are the norms now, not to mention all the makeup.

The pressure of perfectionism manifests as hesitation in decisions, obsession with comparison, and a never-ending dissatisfaction. Perfectionism is a stressor. For those who have a serious case, it can be subtle and not obvious, yet there it dwells within their very nature of everyday interactions and activities.

PERFECTIONISM IN OUR DAILY LIVES

We often practice perfectionism in our daily routines. It can creep up on us in the most trivial ways. For example, in the grocery store we tend to choose the more perfect apple from the produce section. We might obsess over the lines left in the carpet while vacuuming, or similarly the lines in the grass after mowing the lawn. When we shop for clothes, we might become overly concerned with the way a garment fits our body; does it make us look fat? We spend countless hours looking for the perfect outfit for a special occasion.

Our obsession to be perfect can become a subliminal drive as we are exposed to fashion advertising, the latest workout trend, new diets and wellness fads. These sources of the affliction of perfectionism are overt, a constant reminder as they feed perfectionism through all the channels of our lives. It seems that everywhere we look, we are reminded of our imperfections.

By the way, yoga publications and advertising are not exceptions to this. It's very interesting to see the cover shots of yoga publications and yoga apparel manufacturers with the most bendy and skinny models representing all kinds of products, services, and articles. While it's true that no one is forcing us to submit to all this advertising and promotion—we choose to look—it's also true that with the prevalence of technology, by sheer osmosis we are exposed. It's so prevalent that it's like background noise but with an edge. Images of perfect bodies, clothes, poses, etc., become a part of our consciousness, and the need to be perfect becomes a driving force within us. Perfectionism becomes a habit and, like any other habit, can become obsessive to the point of addiction.

Fear comes into play as well. Whether in our professions, activities, or personal lives, the need to be perfect in all that we do causes a fear of being less-than-perfect. This fear can become an inhibiter of freedom, expression, action, and decisiveness. It's also the fear of making a mistake. But if you're not making any mistakes, you are not living and growing.

It's not possible to be mistake-free! For those who are afflicted with this form of perfectionism, it seeps into each and every aspect of their lives, from making travel arrangements to choosing clothes to banking and investment decisions. It can lead to indecisiveness and a lack of engagement in your own life.

PURNAM VS. THE PARADOX

The paradox is that we are perfect as we are. We are born perfect in our own unique way. We all are gifted and are energetic spiritual beings having a temporary human experience. The paradox of perfection reminds us of completeness, fullness, and wholeness.

These are the meanings of the Sanskrit word purnam. The Purnam chant was presented earlier, but here it is again as a reminder. It might be useful if you struggle with perfectionism.

> Om purnamadah, purnamidam
> Purnat purnamudachyate
> Purnasya purnamadaya
> Purnamevavasisyate
> Om Shanti, Shanti, Shanti

As a reminder, the loose translation is, "This is whole, that is whole; from wholeness comes wholeness; that which is left is whole and that which is taken is whole." You can likewise substitute completeness or fullness for wholeness in this chant and it would mean the same.

So here is the paradox: We are originally from wholeness, we are complete, we are full and we are from perfection just as we are. But we forget just how awesome we truly are! Is this another cosmic joke?

You are in fact, perfect as you are!

NAMASTE

Namaste is used as a salutation to greet people or to say goodbye. Greetings and salutations take on a richer form and meaning with this term in its native tongue. It's also used at the beginning or ending of a yoga class by the leader. Translated, it means "I bow to you," or more elaborately, "The divine in me acknowledges and bows to the divine in you."

We love this! For us, this one word captures the essence of our relationships with others. It's so much more meaningful to see with reverence, to see the divine nature of others, and to see yourself in others and them in you. Namaste sets a tone that removes egos and that reminds us we are one and on this earth together. It's a means of union, as we all share this earth, this air, this environment, all of which are living and sacred.

Namaste was a key to unlocking our transformation. When we were so caught up by our corporate consciousness and driven by the acquisition of things, we realized through this one very simple concept that there was another way to view ourselves in this world. If you take this one Sanskrit word, consider its meaning, and allow it to marinate within you, you might find the same as we did. It's a beautiful thing!

HOW YOGA LEADS
TO TRANSFORMATION

"Self-transformation is not just about changing yourself.
It means shifting yourself to a completely new dimension
of experience and perception."
— *Sadhguru*

Over the years we have wondered how yoga worked on us. Our transformation was counter-intuitive, especially as caused by this thing called yoga! Many friends and business associates who knew us as we left our corporate worlds certainly wondered about our mental states and thought we were out of our minds. Well, we might counter with this: Perhaps we were out of our minds during our entire corporate lives. If nothing else, we were certainly caught in a corporate consciousness that clouded our view of the broader aspects of life.

All the wisdom traditions and religions address the need and provide various means to transform ourselves. So many ways presented, and yet most all of us are seemingly lost in the fog of this worldly experience. You are not alone!

From the yogic perspective, transformation is a process of detoxification. The Koshas (remember the Russian doll example?) define the energetic aspects of our being. Each of the layers become poisoned by toxins we encounter and create in our lives. And each is porous, so negative energy can bleed into the neighboring layer. This happens in all aspects of ourselves, from the physical layer through the subtle energetic layers. Our entire system—body, mind, and spirit—requires detoxification so that we can reconnect with our true selves.

As Sadhguru mentions, detoxification for transformation requires shifting to both a new dimension of experience and perception. It's more than just a change of a career or interest. It's shifting your consciousness from the old status quo that you probably complained about but did nothing to change. This is a shift that addresses all aspects of your lifestyle, not just career. It may also include your values, ethics, morals, and view of the world. It's a holistic view.

Attitude, awareness, intention, and mindfulness are all the keys to a meaningful yoga practice. You can go through the motions as though it's just another fitness class, or you can tap into the deeper experience and observe, notice, and take witness of yourself. Even power vinyasa flow at its most challenging and dynamic is a mindful moving meditation.

As avid students, practitioners, and teachers of yoga, we have felt that the *how* of yoga can be mysterious and even elusive. The *what, when*, and *where* of yoga are more obvious. But how yoga works is a question that reaches beyond the teachings themselves. It reaches into the practitioner. How it works lies in the space between yoga as the practice and yoga as the experience *within* the practitioner. As time and practice progress, the difference between yoga and the practitioner fades such that practice is no longer something *done* and becomes a state of being. The lines and boundaries between the practice and the practitioner become blurry.

Our lives are like a whirlwind—or, perhaps, more like a tornado—of tasks, deadlines, texts, emails, work pressures, family responsibilities, and just plain stuff. So much so that we sometimes enter our practice in a fog. Of course, we consciously make the decision to go to yoga practice, but the whirlwind continues even as we arrive: finding an ideal parking spot, checking in, getting the perfect mat placement in the studio, finding your favorite props. The ultimate irony we all have experienced is to rush and plant ourselves on the mat as though we are about to complete just another task from the long to-do list for the day. Yet, this is our chance to literally unplug and metaphorically plug in!

Yoga starts on the mat, but the practice leaves an impression or residual effect. It stays with you. You may not notice this the first or second time you try it, but after several times, yoga interestingly sets up residence in the tissues of your body and the corners of your mind. Its expansion and openness manifest not just as improved range of motion, but also as a limitless spaciousness of the mind.

A complete asana practice follows a flow with defined phases. The beginning of a yoga class might (should) include a centering meditation, perhaps an invocation, and the end should include a final closing chant or a collective Om. These elements are subtle rather than explicit; that is, they are not presented "in your face." They are simply included as part of the practice.

The asanas themselves are hints of a larger story with deeper meaning. They are named after animals, plants, sages, and great teachers. Poses named after plants and animals connect us to nature. Poses named after the great teachers and sages connect us to all who have gone before us and to their traditions. The use of the Sanskrit language—and occasionally chants and seed syllables (Bija Mantras)—yields a deeper connection and meaning. As we've said, *yoga* is translated as *union* or *to yoke*. This is about union of body, mind, and spirit. It's all really beautiful and, we will say, even sacred.

Kathy: Let's explore the word "yoke." You don't hear it much anymore, but most people think of it as to yoke oxen to a cart or horses to a buggy. To yoke with something else (like the oxen or horse) means that it will allow you to go further than you can by yourself. Embracing the principles and techniques of yoga will allow you to go further in life, in your pursuit of happiness, as you stay on the path of enlightenment.

If you are at all open to a deeper experience, perhaps you want to be more mindful, find balance in your life, set an intention to become more peaceful, or dedicate your practice to a loved one in need or who has passed. Then what we call the true essence of yoga will reveal itself. With the right intention we set our direction.

BEING PRESENT REVEALS ALL POSSIBILITIES

An open mind allows for new possibilities. All possibilities exist in the present moment. The past is gone and the future is yet to be. Our ability to shift our perspective and change our world lies within the present moment. To be elsewhere in the continuum of time is to be lost and delusional.

To be open does not have to mean you are all what we call "woo-woo like." *Open* means you allow for even the slightest possibility that there is more at work than your senses sense. That there is more beyond our physical experience that touches our emotions and feelings and can even reach deeper into our inner essence.

Even the slightest openness, just a tiny crack, can reveal new offerings and lessons—just as a window which is partially closed still provides a means for the outside to get in. In yoga, this slight crack of openness correlates to the entry of possibilities, growth, and change beyond just the physical experience of asana alone.

Dennis: The opposite of being open is to be closed, which is a state of being clouded by judgement, assumption, and prejudice. These negative qualities often enter our consciousness in subtle ways, but they are very potent. It is not easy to shift these toward a more positive open view. It begins with an acknowledgement of new possibilities, a willingness to try, and an attitude of allowance. Over time, the present moment becomes what life is all about.

This is part of our story of transformation. In retrospect, being open and willing were key ingredients. Tied with intention, being open and willing creates the right direction, while presence brings forth a channel for all possibilities.

Of course, as with many things in life, transformation or becoming open is not like flipping a switch, where all of a sudden there we are enlightened individuals! It's also not like training for a marathon, where you might lay out a training program and log your miles. We have told our students many times that progress in yoga is measured in millimeters and that you have the rest of your life, so don't rush it. Be open to it and allow for the unseen to reveal itself.

Activating and enabling yoga—by means of practicing and being open— is the essence of turning on yoga as a guidance system for our daily lives. Like a sophisticated navigation technology, yoga becomes the means by which we change our directions through life. This is when we shift from *doing* yoga to *being* yoga.

CONSIDERATIONS FOR YOUR OWN TRANSFORMATION

In our opinion, the key to transformation is patience.

Life is too short…this is true, but why is it that we have to rush everything? Taking a mindful, deliberate approach wins in the long run. This is especially true in transformation.

Usually, transformation requires some sort of significant movement away from your status quo lifestyle, with the operative word here being *significant*. These kinds of significant changes involve various aspects of our own lives, often touch the lives of others, and might involve some risk. So be careful and diligent—but not as a perfectionist, because if you fall into this trap you may never transform.

Meditate. Meditation is very helpful through this process. Not only for stress relaxation, but also for contemplation and inquiry. Allow yourself to sit quietly and shift from a breath-focused meditation into a dialog with your internal guide or guru. This may sound a bit woo-woo for you, but an internal dialog in which you literally ask your guide(s) a question or for guidance in situations can be very revealing.

Do your homework. For example, you might journal about things that bubble up through your newly found awareness. Learn from your aware-ness and take notice of it all. See where you get off track—not just in a physical sense, but emotionally and intellectually.

Ease into simple changes first, the low-hanging fruit so to speak. Build confi-dence in small changes and notice how they support your re-direction.

Tackle the major issues in parallel by doing your due diligence. If it's a career change, you really need to assess your financial situation. Do you need a cash stash to fund your transition? Be truthful with yourself and detailed in your analysis. Transformation is not to be taken casually when it requires major changes. These are life-changing decisions.

We believe that transformation is not a final ending or a destination. It's a process of optimization of self-realization. After all, it's all energy and it all flows. Even once we have taken on a new transformed state of being, we still may need slight adjustments as our lives evolve; in fact, it's very likely. Maintaining mindful awareness with an open attitude and measured discernment will yield this continuous optimization of Self.

Consider the following Apache blessing:

May the sun bring you new energy by day.

May the moon softly restore you by night.

May the rain wash away your worries.

May you walk gently through the world

and know all its beauty, all the days of your life.

THE RIPPLE EFFECT OF YOGA

Imagine a rain drop falling into a pond. Waves radiate from the entry point of that drop as it hits the water's surface. The waves then propagate from the impact point in ever-progressing rings from the center, with diminishing intensity over time and distance. These ripples create change with everything they touch. This ripple effect is also seen in economics, sociology, chemistry, and biology. It's a manifestation of interconnectedness throughout our world and the universe.

Now, consider the ripples created by multiple rain droplets on the pond. Visualize a gentle rain. As each droplet hits the surface of the pond, it radiates waves. These waves interact with the waves of other droplets. This interaction results in either the magnification or cancellation of the waves from the other raindrops. This is fundamental physics, not metaphysics, and not esoteric.

This magnification of waves with equal energies is similar to what happens with certain populations of society, such as groups with common interests and opinions. It creates a momentum—or, let's say, a collective consciousness. This can be good or bad relative to the betterment of society as a whole. Negative examples exist from history throughout the ages—for example, racism or extreme ruling dictators.

The rippling waves of common or unified opinion, values, or actions are additive when they interact and therefore gain power as they radiate. Counteracting these reinforced waves are waves of differing opinion, values, or actions, which offset the opposing waves—hence a cancelling effect that diminishes the energy of opposition. The ripple effect of many can create powerful shifts in consciousness in a society, culture, and even a country.

How does this relate to yoga? Actually, it's fundamental to yoga! Remember, yoga is about relationships. First, you change the relationship with yourself. Then, you radiate this change through your interactions and relationships with others...which in turn touches and changes them. Opportunities to "be the change" and share the change come to us in each moment as we choose actions and reactions that can positively affect the world around us. This is the ripple effect in action through the practice of yoga. Although there is not a chapter in the Yoga Sutras about the ripple effect, it is implied throughout.

Keep in mind, however, that the ripple effect happens no matter what. As energetic beings, we radiate our nature. Positively or negatively, we are creating ripples in the world around us. We are in a constant state of radiance which extends beyond our physicality, beyond our reach, and outward to the universe. You can become the pebble creating the propagation of positive, radiant change in the world.

Everything matters!

LIVE LIFE RAW

It's amazing how yoga has morphed here in the US just since we have found it. There are so many styles, varieties, and blends. That's fine; it's part of the evolution of yoga in today's world in this culture. What is disconcerting, however, are special yoga classes and events which combine drinking alcohol with yoga practice, such as Beer Yoga! Practice yoga while having an ice cold one. Really?

We find this very confusing. It's bad enough people have to go out and hit the bars after a class, but to have it on the mat while practicing is just bizarre. Drinking alcohol is basically about trying to cover up pain and numb the senses. Yoga is just the opposite! We want to *relieve* the emotional pain and *heighten* the senses for increased awareness.

Recall that essentially all of the ancient writings and early teachings of yoga are about the mind. Yoga is about observing the mind, stilling the fluctuations of the mind, calming the mind so that eventually, after lots of practice and focus with the right intention, we drop into Samadhi.

How does a beer contribute? It DOESN'T! We have seen Vino and Vinyasa classes offering wine tasting after a yoga practice. Shouldn't the practice give you a natural, euphoric feeling without the alcohol?

The practice of yoga is to clear the mind, not dull it. We learn about ourselves by cleaning the lens through which we see and cleaning the mirror which reflects our being. We have to face our habits and patterns so that we can have a chance to assess and change.

Here is an idea: Live Life Raw! Face yourself and face your life in the Raw state. As you are, without the fog and distortion caused by mind-altering drugs or alcohol. Be willing to make it part of your practice to be true to yourself *as you are,* without filters. It's the Raw you that will reveal your inner essence.

LIVE SIMPLY, SIMPLY LIVE

Kathy: I like to tell our yoga students that we spend the first half of our lives "inhaling"—meaning getting an education, acquiring a job, house, career, and material things. Then, at some point, and not a specific age, we begin to "exhale," downsize, be content with less, and realize what's important in the big scheme of things.

We started to exhale around the age of forty-seven or so, but I have seen some folks exhale in their thirties, and others who never really exhale but instead spend their whole lives thinking that material things or more money will make them happy— "When I get this next big promotion or when I can afford a certain car or live in that neighborhood, I will have made it and then I will be happy."

But what these folks are missing is that everything in life is just borrowed. You don't really own anything. That fancy car? You'll only have it for a certain number of years. Same with the house. Your clothes will be recycled as you buy new ones. Even our breath is borrowed. We inhale, and then we give it back. The proof is that not one of us leaves this planet alive, and we can't take anything with us, so while we are here, everything is simply borrowed.

Dennis: Growing up in these times and in this culture, it seems that we are taught to lean into life. As we lean into life, we tend to have a bias toward saying yes too much and we tend to be more reactive than responsive. This combination of leaning into life, over-extending ourselves, and pulling triggers too fast results in making our lives complex. Suddenly we feel the force or the headwind. We are stressed out and eventually burned out from the complexity of our lives. It's like a salmon swimming upstream against the current. We tax our systems, cortisol levels run high and long, exhaustion kicks in, we become short-tempered and out of balance. But is it all real or contrived by us?

This is a rhetorical question. Yes, we place ourselves under these pressures. Consider leaning back as life passes. I do not mean going passive and disengaging; I mean shift into a mindful awareness that allows you to assess and respond. Be alive in the moments of your life, experience life raw, as pure as it is. As we lean back, even a little, our lives become a little less hectic, a little more balanced, and we feel more connected to presence. Dr. Scott Blossom, a beautiful Ayurvedic practitioner, says that twenty percent of illnesses can be avoided if we simply do less.

We live moment to moment, always within a set state of consciousness. As we grow, evolve, and experience life, our consciousness can evolve into a new set point or state. In other words, our consciousness can be passively defined or it can be actively created and molded. We can shift it with our intention.

Consciousness is coupled with our overall sense of well-being and happiness. It's all connected! To use the yogic view, our *bodies* are the accumulation of the food we eat and our *minds* are the accumulation of impressions in our lives. Food and impressions either nourish our lives for a long sustainable and happy experience—or they don't. Using us as an example, our previous corporate consciousness served us well for a while until it became out of balance. We were not happy and, correspondingly, our well-being suffered. Yoga allowed us to shift our consciousness into a new set point and see things from a different perspective.

As we move through our lives, we create a frame of reference which is psychological, based upon assumptions and perceptions that define a consciousness set point for how we think we feel, interact, and experience the world. This perceived sense of health, happiness, and wellness can be blurred and even delusional when we are out of balance, overstressed, or out of harmony with nature or our purpose in life. We can become satisfied with the status quo of a comfort zone which is actually not sustainable and, over time, is even detrimental to our lives. The comfort zone is a beautiful place to be, but there is no growth there.

Lean back, make space, live simply, and simply live.

IMPRESSIONS

As we live our lives, we create energetic impressions upon others. All of our interactions with others project our feelings, our thoughts, our moods—or more generally, our energy—upon them. Our body language and facial expressions speak for themselves as visible indicators of our emotional and energetic state in the moment. These interpersonal impressions can be positive, negative, or neutral and can create long-lasting residual energies. As they say, there is only one chance for a first impression.

Our embodied, physical being leaves impressions in the form of footprints in the ground as we propel ourselves across the earth. One day we were on a long meditative walk on the beach, when we could not help but notice the differences in our respective footprints in the sand: their depth relating to our individual weight and style of walking, their geometry relating to the size and shape differences of our feet. These footprint impressions would remain until the next wave washed them away. A short-lived but real residual effect.

Similarly, we spoke of impressions left on our yoga mats. The scrapes and tears are evidence of our practices, unique to each of us like our signatures or fingerprints. We propel ourselves across many surfaces in life, leaving behind signs of our passing through.

Words are powerful impressions, as once they leave our mouths there is no return. If regret follows, then remorse and apology are the only forms of recourse to heal any negative impact. Words of the English language can have multiple meanings. Our choice of words and how we express them, our emphasis, adds color to the meaning and interpretation of our words.

There is an old practice that's been handed down from long ago, in which we consider and filter our words first before speaking. The filter is a series of three questions:

- Is what we want to say kind?
- Is it true?
- Is it necessary?

What if we all adopted this practice? How would the world be different? How would politics be different? Even if we each chose a single of these questions as a filter, communications would be improved. The point is to pause first.

Let's look at the word *light*. As a noun, light is energy. As an adjective, light describes luminescence. As energetic beings, *we* are light and can shine our light. We radiate and share our energies simply by existing. In the yogic conceptual model of the body, we are composed of energetic layers and we radiate electro-magnetic, thermal, acoustic, and other forms of energy. So the question becomes, what is the nature of the energy we emit? Is it positive or negative?

Light can also refer to our weight, both literal and metaphorical, as we walk the earth and leave a physical imprint. The weight of our lives bears down on the earth via gravity and by means of our style of life. Consider your style of life. Are you living in harmony with nature? What is the impact of your lifestyle on your friends, neighbors, and community? Are you considerate of others? It's arrogant and inappropriate to live at the expense of others, where *expense* means any form of negative impact—physical, mental, emotional, or energetic—on any being, sentient or not.

One of our favorite quotes is:

> *"Live light, travel light, spread the light, be the light."*
> — *Yogi Bhajan*

Unconscious impressions are the most concerning, as these are just as real and at least as impactful as conscious ones, but come from a place of mindlessness. Some examples are:

- Interrupting others during a conversation
- Snapping to judgement based upon false assumptions
- Lack of sensitivity or empathy for others
- Mindless, disconnected listening
- Texting while driving, conversing, or eating
- Trying to multi-task while in the presence of others

Be willing to observe all your interactions and how your life affects others, including all beings and the world around you. Notice this with an open mind, and then, with truthfulness, ask yourself the following questions:

- Are any of my words or actions hurting my loved ones, friends, or associates?
- Are my actions having a negative impact on the planet?
- Are these actions or words in alignment with my moral and ethical values?
- What is the cost to others of my actions or my lifestyle?
- Are these actions or words supportive of my roles in life?
- Even though I was present, did I uplift the present moment?

It's not easy to minimize our impact and negative impressions in all aspects of our lives, physically and energetically. But why not start now and see how you can shift your world?

LIVING ON PURPOSE WITH PURPOSE

It's a part of our nature to live with purpose. As sentient beings with high intellect, we naturally want to lead happy and fulfilling lives. There is a tendency, however, to be drawn deeply into the vortex of everyday life like a tornado that generates a vacuum. When this happens, it's as though we go through the motions of life with a sort of mindless momentum, living life without really being there.

The ancient concept of *dharma* is defined as *cosmic or universal law*. Purpose, as we mean it, is living in full expression of your intrinsic nature that is also in harmony with the universe; that is, taking the right actions that are in support of the greater good and the universe as a whole. In other words, living your dharma. Sometimes this can seem elusive and intimidating. Thankfully, contemplative practices like yoga, meditation, and Qi Gong exist and can help us reconnect to our inner essence.

We each came to this earth with an essence that lies dormant deep within us. It's covered under a veil that distorts and obstructs our view, a veil woven of past issues, past karmas, traumas, negative thoughts, emotions, feelings, and even concerns of the future. This barrier is created by us. It's inherited via our ancestors, it's tribal via our culture, and it has a national component via our citizenship. But under this veil lies our inner essence, home to our true purpose and our unique gifts.

The sad truth is that most all of us miss it. We cannot see it, or hear it, or sense it, because the veil of distortion blocks our view. Many of us will live our entire lives having not connected to this essence and therefore having missed the precious chance to express it. When we find ourselves in this mode of just skimming across the surface of life, like a skipping stone tossed across the surface of a pond, we miss the beauty of what lies below the surface.

> *Dennis*: This idea of a mindless autopilot mode is the best way for me to describe myself from my own experience. In my previous consciousness, I was successful in many ways but missing on so many levels. Honestly, I think I had let the intellect of my brain get in the way of the wisdom of my heart. I had forgotten who I was. Or maybe it was my upbringing, my tribe, or inherited past karmas that clouded my view and awareness. You see, when my cousin Lori planted her "current consciousness" seed, I did not know that consciousness was rooted to our inner essence.
>
> Living life with wholeness, with fearlessness, in harmony with nature, and in alignment with the universe is to live life with full and complete consciousness, not the filtered and distorted consciousness that I lived for so many years.

It's easy to live in opposition or out of alignment with the universe or our dharma. With the speed of life today, our apparent need to keep up consumes us. Soon we lose touch with ourselves. Maybe we are very successful and very good at leaning into life. But, after a while, maybe ten years or maybe thirty, we might look around and wonder where time went, feeling as though we're missing something but can't quite put our finger on what it is.

Health, happiness, and longevity are the three elements of making life worth living. The interesting thing about these three qualities is that they are interconnected as well. If you are unhappy, your health will suffer and so will longevity. If you are unhealthy, you will not be happy and, likewise, your longevity will be limited.

We all want longevity. Of course, it's possible to live a happy and healthy life that's cut short due to accidental passing or divine calling. But we all want to create a legacy for when we leave this earth. Health and happiness are the keys, but they are dependent upon our authenticity, openness, and willingness to live in harmony with nature, the world, and the universe: our dharma.

THE ANNIVERSARY OF YOUR DEATH

Although this may strike you as a morbid concept, hang with us for just a bit. Bhutan, a country in the Himalayas, is found to be the happiest place in the world. A daily practice of many citizens of Bhutan is to meditate upon their deaths, which is an ancient Buddhist meditation practice. It's not morbid and certainly not intended to depress you; in fact, it's quite the opposite.

> *Dennis*: Many years ago we came across this poem about the anniversary of your death.

> For the Anniversary of My Death
> by W. S. Merwin (Merwin, 1993)

> Every year without knowing it I have passed the day
> When the last fires will wave to me
> And the silence will set out
> Tireless traveler
> Like the beam of a lightless star

Then I will no longer
Find myself in life as in a strange garment
Surprised at the earth
And the love of one woman ...

There are a few more lines to the poem but it's a beautiful reminder of our mortality. It's so profound thinking
about the fact that every year we are alive, we not only
live through the anniversary of our birth, but also of
our day of passing, the anniversary of our death.

Each day we live could be the day in which we pass the
next year. So the question to ourselves is: What if this were
true? How would you live your life if you only had a year
left? To say nothing of what if this were your last day?

The practices of death meditation and the awareness of living through
the anniversary of your passing can be very liberating. We in the West
tend to shuffle the elderly aside and sidestep the reality of death. Guess
what? From the day you were born you are dying. You have an expiration
date, but it's unknown. The unknown is part of the mystery of life.

Another lesson learned is the very challenging art of letting go. At some point
you will have no choice but to let go. We become so attached to our possessions,
titles, and perceived importance. The problem with this so-called possession is
it's temporary. For us, this was an important lesson: impermanence.

These two lessons are tied to one another as we MUST learn to let go, as
all things are impermanent. It's all energy! Remember?

So our time here is limited; therefore, we need to make the most of the
time we have.

IT'S NEVER TOO LATE

We are just a heartbeat away from passing and going on to our next assignment. No matter what age you are, you have no idea how much longer you have. It's never too late. Even a short time with a harmonized purpose is a life of potency, one that can leave this earth a better place than when you arrived.

This ancient Zen saying sums this up:

> *In the end, what matters most is:*
> *How well did you live,*
> *How well did you love,*
> *How well did you learn to let go.*

FOR COUPLES AND PARTNERS

When we first met, it was so obvious and natural that we were meant to be together. It was as though we already knew each other. Over the years, we have often referred to each other as soulmates. Having had past-life regression sessions as well as readings from mediums and shamans, we have been told we were together in many past lives.

Even so, we have faced challenges and difficulties along the way, just like any other couple. As we would reflect upon our journey and its twists and turns, our yoga practices reinforced the cornerstones for us: love, gratitude, communication, compromise, compassion, and a heavy touch of reverence.

- Love is first and foremost. Unconditional love from the heart. This is the kind of love that will not quit and is everlasting, no matter what the issue or challenge. Love conquers all. Without love, the other cornerstones don't have a chance.
- Gratitude is the nectar that adds that extra special taste or essence to a relationship. To be grateful for everything you have together and grateful for each other.
- Communication and compromise go hand-in-hand. We all want it our way—but seriously, so do all the other billions of people on the planet! We all must compromise and cooperate, especially with our life partners. To do otherwise is to plant seeds of resentment which

grow aggressively like weeds.

- Compassion comes from the heart. It's linked to our empathetic selves in which we learn to see from the eyes of others as well as feel and sense from their perspective.
- Reverence places emphasis on the awesomeness and profound nature of the relationship, the other individual, and the world in which you live. It's all to be revered, as it's all so incredible that words fall short. Consider how precious and how fragile life is and realize that each moment shared is truly a gift.

We are blessed to have a relationship with a strong foundation in love, that came from a place of compromise and a willingness to be open and change together, grow together, and go with the flow. It was not until much later in our time together that we would learn what going with the flow really meant and how our journey together would lead us to such an awesome life.

BURN THROUGH THE DELUSION WITH LOVE

When you boil it all down and take a closer look at life, we live within a delusion of our own creation. Within a lifestyle as partners or couples, the many issues we face and burdens we carry are a consequence of delusion. So many folks today are unhappy and struggle through life trying to seek happiness from all the wrong places and for all the wrong reasons. Whether it's issues with material things, money, bad relationships or addictions, our habits and patterns can be linked to issues of love.

Consider the relationships of yoga. Recall, there are four: you with yourself, you with others, you with the world around you, and you with spirit.

First, let's look at our relationship with our self. So many of our own issues are direct fallout of not loving ourselves. When we talk of loving ourselves, we mean *self-love* in terms of our own happiness and well-being, a love of self which is sincere, nurturing, and heart centered— not narcissistic self-love, which is driven by an out-of-balance ego. Self-love is absolutely necessary and really comes first, as you cannot give that which you do not have. Our love for others is a reflection of our self-love. If you try to give love without a healthy sense of self-love, then it's likely not sustainable in the long term, or sincere.

Let's combine love for others with love for the world around you. Of course you love your partner or spouse in a different way than you love your dog or chocolate. As a side note, perhaps we here in the US, with English as our primary language, are at a disadvantage when it comes to love. Hang with us for just a minute. The Sanskrit language has ninety-six words for love. Ancient Persian has eighty. Greek has three. In English, we have only one (HuffPost, The Blog, 7/4/2012). But this one word can't possibly cover all the kinds of love; after all, we can love more than one individual, and in several different ways. Have you noticed how more people say "I love you" today to friends, not just reserving that one word for just one person?

Our relationship with spirit, universe, or God is another love. To us, this is the truest of love. Interestingly, this love also can be found inside us within the Anandamaya Kosha, the layer of our innermost blissful self. Self-love is a derivative of this love, as from love of the spirit comes all other love. Therefore, to love yourself truly is a reflection of love of spirit, universe, or God, and it opens you to love others as you love yourself.

As M.C. Yogi says, "Only love is real." Love transcends all. Love is the source, the power, and the reason to be here. To find love, to be love, and to share love, we must first of all love ourselves.

FINDING FUN, MAKING MEMORIES

In our early days together we came up with this mantra for our lives together. *Finding fun, making memories* has been the underlying theme of our thirty-five-plus years together.

In the beginning of our journey together, we must have had some intuitive connection to this phrase as it aligns with what leads to true happiness on earth. We are here to learn, enjoy, and contribute. *Finding fun, making memories* has kept us focused less on the materialistic and more on the things that really matter in life.

Yes, everything matters.

FOR TEACHERS

Based on our experience, our practices, and the reflections presented herein, we want to share the following nuggets that might be useful to other teachers. Here are the keys we feel are essential for yoga teachers:

- Be your best authentic self
- Create a sacred space and hold it
- Teach only that which you practice
- Do not take yourself so seriously
- Bring depth and richness to each class (don't just be a fitness instructor)
- Recognize that the practice is a sacred and healing modality
- Remember that to be a yoga teacher is a responsibility
- Acknowledge that you are making a difference and touching lives
- Realize that your students are counting on you
- Accept that the world is counting on you! (Feel no pressure! As a yoga teacher, you are a guide, leader, holistic healer, consultant…just to mention a few of the roles you play!)

IN THE END

Nature is cyclic. Nature does not worry or force, she just is. Our breath comes and goes in waves, as an inhalation and a pause at the top followed by the exhalation and a pause at the bottom. Each moment flows one into another. What if the cycles of nature, the cycles of our breath, and the flow of the moments within our lives are the hidden keys or hints of what can be magical transitions?

Transitions are inevitable. Impermanence is an absolute of our life here in this earthly existence, and impermanence initiates and leads to transitions. Therefore our happiness relies upon acknowledging, accepting, and embracing impermanence, and mindfully expressing our transitions. All endings bring new beginnings. Future generations learn from those who have gone before them, just as we have. The ancestral chain passes on wisdom via transitions generation to generation.

Everything matters in all aspects of our lives. There is nothing that does not matter in this lifetime. Our lives are interconnected, interdependent, and influence all who are on this earth and even the earth herself. Therefore, we must live life fully aware, fully empowered, and fully responsible for the betterment of all beings in this world. This isn't meant to be a burden or drive us into a paranoid state of living. We are here on earth to learn, to love, and to serve.

"Everything matters" is not a pessimistic view, it's an empowered, positive view. Through our travels we meet so many people from so many countries in our workshops and retreats, and we see the potential for a positive shift in the world. We are especially hopeful for and optimistic about future generations as they have had ours to observe and learn from.

When you stand on a beach at the edge of the ocean and you gaze to the horizon where the sky meets the earth, you are only about three miles away from that horizon. Not long ago, that same horizon was thought to be the edge of the earth, beyond which there was nothing. The earth was believed to be flat. The reality of course, as we now know, is that the earth is spherical, with a circumference of nearly 25,000 miles. Just the ratio of these distances reveals that assuming the earth was flat and the view to the horizon was all there was, we would have missed 99.98% of what actually lies beyond.

Our view and understanding of our world and the universe is limited by our perceptions and biological limitations, but today's science and technologies are pushing our horizons far beyond what is seen or perceived through our senses. Amazingly, the universe is both larger and infinitesimally smaller than our capabilities to measure even today. Whether toward the infinite or the infinitesimal, the unseen is where the unknown lies.

In many ways for us, it was the technology and practices of yoga that revealed the unseen within each of us and us as a couple. We became our own subjects of study and investigation.

And it all comes down to the one main lesson: the REAL TRUTH.

Everything matters.

Peace, Joy, Love, and Light!

ACKNOWLEDGEMENTS

Whether we live to be 80, 100, or even 108 years old, our time here on earth is very limited. We are thankful to all who have gone before us and thankful to be alive right now. We are grateful to you for buying this book for a deeper view into our story.

A huge thank you to our many teachers along the way who helped us realize the importance of taking the path less chosen: Kate Cordell, our first yoga teacher, who had copious amounts of patience with us; Stephanie Keach for giving us 500+ hours of the best yoga teacher training on the planet; Terese Whitley, Adam Rice, and Ashley Davies for keeping us on the path; Dr. Keith Holden for introducing us to the magic of crystal bowls and his positive energy; Dr. Shauna Shapiro for her warm heart, teachings, guidance and friendship; the masterful teachings of Erich Schiffmann, Rodney Yee, Jai Uttal, Luna Ray, Gurmukh Kaur Khalsa, and Shiva Rea, for all of their wisdom of the ancient teachings that helped shaped us; Paul Grilley, Sarah Powers, and Shala Worsley for helping us fall in love with Yin Yoga; David Life and Sharon Gannon for their powerful views on veganism which convinced us to adopt a strict vegan diet in 2005; Cora Wen for showing us the merits and beauty of Restorative Yoga; Michael Singer and his insightful talks at the Temple of the Universe; Ruth Hartung (Sraddhasagar) of the 7 Centers Yoga Arts in Sedona, Arizona for introducing us to Kundalini Tantra Yoga, and to the legacy of Yogi Bhajan for bringing the teachings of Kundalini Yoga to the US as he shared the light.

And most recently, lastly but certainly not the least, we are so very thankful and grateful to Lori Snyder of Yoga:edit for her encouragement, guidance, and limitless patience as she led us in completing this book. Without her this would not have come together.

Om Shanti to you all!

ABOUT THE COVER

Matthew Morse, the designer for this book, chose the idea of origami—the art of folding paper into sculptures—as a symbol for our cover. Each piece of the cover image represents a piece of our experience. The birds themselves are us; the folds and creases that create each bird stand for our individual change and growth; the color blue shows our deep union throughout these transformations; the threads supporting the birds depict our connection to all that is around us. We simply love this vision, which we feel captures the essence of our book. They say a picture is worth a thousand words—or, as is the case here, more like 60,000!

REFERENCES

Bryant, Edwin F. *The Yoga Sutras of Patanjali.* North Point Press, 2009.

Burnes, Deborah. "Putting It On Your Skin Lets It In: What's In Skin Care and How It Affects You." Huffington Post, June 21, 2012, www.huffingtonpost.com/deborah-burnes/skin-care_b_1540929.html.

Dale, Cyndi. *The Subtle Body: An Encyclopedia of Your Energetic Anatomy.* Sounds True, 2009.

Davis, Bruce, PhD. "There Are 50,000 Thoughts Standing Between You and Your Partner Every Day." Huffington Post, May 23, 2013. https://www.huffingtonpost.com/bruce-davis-phd/healthy-relationships_b_3307916.html.

Easwaran, Eknath. *The Upanishads.* Nilgiri Press, 2007.

Feuerstein, Georg. *The Deeper Dimension of Yoga. Shambala, 2003.*

Grilley, Paul. *Yin Yoga: Principles and Practices, 10th Anniversary Edition.* White Cloud Press, 2012.

Harari, Yuval Noah. *Sapiens: A Brief History of Humankind.* HarperCollins, 2015.

Hawkins, David R. *Power Vs. Force: The Hidden Determinants of Human Behaviors.* Hay House Inc., 1995.

Jobs, Steve. Stanford 2005 Commencement Speech. Stanford University, June 2005. www.news.stanford.edu/2005/06/14/jobs-061505/.

Kabat-Zinn, Jon. *Wherever You Go, There You Are, 10th Anniversary Edition.* Hyperion Books, 2015.

Lang, Kathy. "What 108 means To Me." Natural Awakenings: Northeast Florida Edition, November 2008.

Lazar, Sara. "Harvard Neuroscientist: Meditation Not Only Reduces Stress, Here's How it Changes Your Brain." *The Washington Post,* May 26, 2015. www.washingtonpost.com/news/inspired-life/wp/2015/05/26/harvard-neuroscientist-meditation-not-only-reduces-stress-it-literally-changes-your-brain/?utm_term=.f34f98301206

Merwin, W.S. *The Second Four Books of Poems.* Copper Canyon Press, 1993.

Ming-Dao, Deng. *365 Tao: Daily Meditations.* Harper One, 1992.

Mitchell, Stephen. *The Bhagavad Gita.* Three Rivers Press, 2002 translation.

Muktibodhananda. *Hatha Yoga Pradipika.* Yoga Publications Trust, 1992 translation.

Paul, Sheryl. "96 Words For Love." Huffington Post, July 4, 2012. www.huffingtonpost.com/sheryl-paul/96-words-for-love_b_1644658.html.

Schiffmann, Erich. *Yoga: The Spirit of Moving Into Stillness.* Pocket Books, 1996.

Shaw, Edwina. "How Toning The Vagus Nerve Heals Pain." upliftconnect.com, November 3, 2017. upliftconnect.com/toning-vagus-nerve-heals-pain/.

Sturgess, Stephen. *Raja & Kriya Yoga: The Ultimate Path to Self-Realization.* Singing Press, 2005.

White, Ganga. *Yoga Beyond Belief: Insights to Awaken and Deepen Your Practice.* North Atlantic Books, 2007.

Zukav, Gary. *The Seat of the Soul.* Touchstone/Fireside, Simon & Schuster, 1990.

APPENDIX 1:
OUR FAVORITE MANTRAS

We are as much mantra yogis as we are Vinyasa, Kundalini, and Yin yogis. Here is a partial list of our favorite mantras with a brief commentary. The translations are casual, but the meanings are on target.

- Gayatri Mantra: Perhaps the oldest of all recorded mantras, said to be the mantra of mantras. The Gayatri is an acknowledgment of and meditation on the life-giving qualities of the sun, which provides light, warmth, and prana to the entire universe, indiscriminately. It provides life for all beings, regardless of species, demographics, or lifestyle. This is an unconditional love, with no catch. The purpose of meditating on the Gayatri is not only to be thankful but, more importantly, to take on these same qualities in our own daily lives. We should each share our warmth and light, without discrimination or attachments, with all beings, no matter who, what, when, or where.

Om Bhuh Bhuvaha Swaha
Om Tat Savitur Varenyum
Bhargo Devasya Dhimahi
Dhiyo Yonaha Prachodayat

- *Purnam:* The prelude chant to the Brihadaranyaka Upanishad, this chant provides comfort and strength to know that all is full, complete, and perfect.

Om Purnamadah Purnamidam
Purnat purnam udachyate
Purnasya purnumadaya
Purnamevavashishyate
Om, Shanti, Shanti, Shanti

- *Lokah Samashta Sukinuno Bhavantu:* Considered the anthem of yoga, the Lokah (or Peace chant) has become very popular. This chant is a prayer for peace, peace for ALL beings in all realms. It translates as, *May all beings find happiness and peace, and may my/our own actions contribute to that happiness and peace.*

- *Om Gum Ganapataya Namaha:* This is one we have used for our travels and road trips, and we have chanted this literally thousands of times over thousands of miles. This mantra taps into the qualities of the Hindu God Ganesha as the remover of obstacles. It calls his name twice: once as the seed syllable *Gum* and then with his full name, *Ganapatayei.* As it begins with the primordial sound of Om, it evokes salutations to petition for the removal of obstacles in our lives. *Namaha* seals it all in his name.

- *Om Mani Padme Hum: The jewel lies within the lotus.* As we apply this, the jewel is our inner essence or light, which has qualities like the sun and resides deep within our heart as represented by the lotus of the Anahata chakra center. The chant is a reminder to shine our light with the world.

- *Ra Ma Da Sa Sa Say So Hung:* This is a mantra of the Kundalini Yoga tradition in the language of Gurmukhi. It's a healing chant that can be used for yourself or others. This chant's direct meaning is tied to the energies of the universe, with the infinite and the infinitesimal universal energies coalescing and focusing power for healing. It also can be applied to a chakra balancing practice, in which each syllable corresponds to the balance qualities of each charka starting at the base and progressing up the spine. Notice that *Sa* is said twice, as Anahata chakra, the heart center, is the transitional center between the bottom three chakras of our worldly selves and the upper three chakras of our universal selves.

- *Om:* The all-encompassing and primordial sound of the universe. The entire Mandukya Upanishad is dedicated to Om, it's so important! We chant *Om* as we "charge" our food before eating and then chant *Jai!* This is our blessing for our food and for victory (meaning praise, acknowledgment, and thanks) for the chef, the farmers, the store employees, and all the hands that came together for the preparation of our meal.

- *Om Shanti, Shanti, Shanti:* A mantra of peace, this chant is not only beautiful but also powerful. The first *shanti* is recited to invoke peace within yourself, the second *shanti* is for peace in your family and community, and the last is chanted for peace in the world.

APPENDIX 2:
SEVERAL MEDITATIONS

The following meditations are guided relaxations which are available for free via our Soundcloud link on our website, yogawithdennisandkathy.com. In addition to guided meditations, you can also find our meditative instrumental music there.

You can use the meditations provided here mentally, without audio playback, or in conjunction with the recordings. Guiding yourself mentally is a very good form of self-guided relaxation.

1. Spatial Meditation

In a comfortable seated position with a straight spine,
Soften your breath, slow it down, with emphasis on the exhalation.
Avoid the tendency to rush the breath; use long, slow, deep, easy breathing.
Soften your shoulders, your face, your brow.
Soften your thoughts, emotions, and mind.

Acknowledge the space around you
Notice all that surrounds you with all the senses
What do you hear?
Do you feel a breeze?
Do you feel a temperature?

Is there a taste or is there a smell?
What do you see through your mind's eye?
Do you see your surroundings, can you visualize the space?
Notice, allow to simply be with no judgment.
Allow all to be that which surrounds you.

Now bring your awareness to self, your physical self.
Can you feel the shape of your posture?
Do you feel the contact you make with the chair or cushion that supports you?
Can you feel the earth below supporting you?
Can you feel your perimeter, the outer boundaries of your physical self?
Can you sense and feel your body, its structure, its organs, tissues, and fluids?

Now let your awareness progress deeper.
Deeper to the non-physical, to your emotional self.
Notice your thoughts and feelings, simply observe them, allow them to
pass as though they are clouds in the sky.

Go deeper still
To your mental self.
Notice there are no boundaries here within the mental self.
Notice you are not your thoughts, as they have passed.
Notice your emotions were but momentary responses from the exterior.

Your mind is vast, it's spacious, it has no limits as with the exterior,
the mind has no boundaries, it is yours, and it is you.

Scan across yourself, all of yourself, all the layers of your being.
You are perfection, you are perfect as you are,
you always have been and always will be.

2. Ocean Wave Yoga Nidra

As you lie on your back, soften and release.

Allow gravity to have you.

Let the systems and tissues of your body release, soften your breath.

Let the thoughts go, and out to the corners of your mind release into a sleepless sleep.

Now imagine you are transported to a soft, sandy beach, lying next to the ocean's edge.

You hear waves as they caress the beach.

You smell the ocean air.

You feel a gentle breeze as it passes over you,

you hear gulls playing in the distance,

you feel the sun's glowing warmth as it radiates and penetrates your body.

Your eyes are closed but your mind's eye sees the yellow,

glowing sun above.

You are at one with nature and it is at one with you.

As you continue to release and relax, notice an energetic wave form at the bottoms of your feet.

This wave is special as it brings warm, moist, penetrating relaxation and healing touch to all the tissues and cells of your body.

It enlightens and enlivens each molecule of you that it touches.

The wave continues from the bottoms of the feet, passing over the shins and up to the knees. You notice the soft, healing stillness and relaxation, the legs soften deeper into the warm sand beneath you with a pause, you hear the ocean waves, feel the gentle breeze, feel the warmth of the sun and hear the gulls in the distance.

You at one with nature.

The wave continues up the thighs, you feel the quadriceps release, the hamstrings release.

The wave continues up over the hips and pauses at the waist.

Your legs soften deeper into the sand, they open wider as gravity takes them. The breeze passes over you, you smell the ocean air.

The wave continues up over the torso, pausing at the shoulders.

You notice the spine as pearls on a string, releasing each vertebra into the sand. All the organs release, the intercostal muscles between your ribs release,

your shoulders release, the arms fall open as they soften deeper into the sand.

With a pause, you hear the ocean waves, feel the gentle breeze, feel the warmth of the sun and hear the gulls in the distance.

You are at one with nature.

The wave continues along your body.

Passing over the neck it transmits warm, radiant, healing energy to your throat, the thyroid, and the cervical spine.

The wave continues over the face, your jaw softens, the tongue softens, your expression softens, your brow softens.

The wave continues to the top, to the crown of your head. It pauses.

You visualize a glowing white energy that encompasses your entire body, it radiates with a pulsating, vibrating massage on a cellular level throughout you,

all of you, your physical self, your emotional self, your mental self.

It massages and transmits its healing energy into and through all aspects of you.

The wave then passes back across the full length of your body, receding
and returning from where it came.
Leaving you behind in complete and total relaxation.
At one with yourself, at one with nature, at one with all.

3. Meandering and Merging into Blues

As you lie on your back, release and relax, soften your breath.
Imagine you are floating on top of water, a moving and flowing body of water.

This water is buoyant with its superior minerals and healing qualities, the
water is warm, its temperature matches yours; there is no difference.

It's moist, it's soft, its buoyancy supports you, all of you, your physical self,
emotional self, and mental self; all of you, it holds you in its grasp.

This body of water flows as an estuary, passing from within valleys of
the forest toward the ocean.
The journey meanders and flows; you are with it as one,
you are a passenger.
You are in deep relaxation but aware of this flowing journey, you feel
the gentle caress of soft waves.

You notice the clear blue sky above with its warm glowing sun.
Beyond the water's edge and within the valley is the forest.

You hear wildlife in the distance as you pass by, floating on the current,
going with the flow.

During this journey, the thoughts are few, and fewer.
Your mind opening to clear, meditative skies.

The water supports you as it flows along the estuary.
You smell the clean air, you hear the forest in the near distance.

You are flowing as a river toward the ocean, with no hesitation, no worries.
You pass by obstructions as you go with the flow.
Your emotions release into the flow.
You are washed clean of negative energy that does not serve you.

The journey continues as you float,
meandering gently and slowly to the ocean's edge,
where the tide meets the river,
where your spirit meets your mind and body.

Your awareness expands and the finite river becomes the infinite ocean
your awareness is beyond awareness of your body floating in the water
It's beyond the feelings of buoyancy, motion, and thought
beyond the five senses as you float past the tidal boundary at the edge of
the estuary as the journey takes you deeper into the ocean

The ocean's surface is gentle, soft, and glassy, its deep blue reflects the
sky, the radiance of the sun.

You continue where the ocean and sky merge.
In the vastness near the horizon, flowing motion feels like stillness.
You float, floating between the blues, surrounded by the blue of the
ocean's water supporting you and the blue of the sky above.
At the horizon, these blues merge in the distance, they become one.
You become one, you merge as blues merge within you.

As you remain in deep relaxation, you are merged with the energetic
healing blues of the ocean and sky.
A sense of deep healing, deep relaxing and releasing pulsates within and
throughout you.

4. Letting Go: A Meditative Contemplation (Parable)

There's an ancient story from China about monkeys, coconuts, and rice. The villagers would hollow out a coconut, leaving an opening barely the size of a monkey's hand. Inside the coconut, they would put rice. Then when the sun began to set, they would place the coconuts along the path where the monkeys liked to run. When it got dark, the monkeys would come around and smell the rice. They would put their hand in the opening of the coconut and grab the rice. But to their surprise, their rice-filled and clenched hand would no longer fit through the hole!

The monkeys who were caught were those who would not let go of the rice. So long as the monkey held onto the rice, they were a prisoner of their own making. All they had to do to be free was let go of the rice, but many monkeys would not do that. The coconut trap worked because the monkeys, at that moment, believed they would not be able to find food anywhere else and would cling to the rice.

The lesson for us is that maybe we are holding onto something that is making us a prisoner or unhappy. Maybe you think that your job is the only one you'll ever find? Or your partner is the only one who will love you? Maybe you are keeping your children in a tight grip?

What is your rice? Do you really need to hang on so tightly? And what is that hanging-on keeping you from?

If you open your fist, you will be amazed at the opportunities that will come your way. So much more can happen if we can go through life with open hands instead of clenched fists. Keeping a tight grip is often just the thing that keeps us stuck—though we want to blame everything else, especially what we are holding onto.

ABOUT THE AUTHORS

Dennis and Kathy Lang are husband and wife, together since 1982. Yoga found them back in 2000 at the Miraval Spa resort in Arizona. They are both certified E-RYT500 / YACEP teachers of yoga, meditation, and mindfulness. Dennis also holds a BS and MS in Structural Engineering from the University of Massachusetts, Amherst, and Kathy holds a BS in Business from Clemson University. After twenty-four years in the corporate world in various middle and upper management roles, they voluntarily retired themselves to pursue their new career path as yoga and meditation teachers.

Both Dennis and Kathy are legacy ambassadors with Lululemon Athletica. As ethereal musicians, they integrate sound and vibration into their teaching as a healing modality with Spanish guitar, fusion sitar, crystal bowls, gong, Native American flute, harmonium, drums, and chimes.

Students say, "Practicing yoga with them is a magical blend of mindfulness, placid vibrational sound, and live acoustic music created to accompany their warm and down-to-earth teaching style. They pay attention to all aspects and dimensions of what yoga is really about. This is a practice where every soul can sing, every heart can open, the noise can cease, and every body can know its own beauty."

Annually, Dennis and Kathy lead more than forty workshops and teacher trainings in the US, plus retreats overseas. Their foundations are in Vinyasa Flow, Kundalini, Yin, and Mantra yoga, but they also specialized in Chakra Theory, Energetic Anatomy, and holistic healing. As lovers of adventure and other cultures, they have traveled to nearly forty countries and their lifelong mantra is "finding fun and making memories."

For more on them and their teaching programs, retreats, music, and meditations, please visit www.yogawithdennisandkathy.com.

69134103R00154

Made in the USA
Columbia, SC
14 August 2019